The Shaman
and the
Medicine Wheel

The Shaman and the Medicine Wheel

By Evelyn Eaton
(Mahad'yuni)

The Theosophical Publishing House
Wheaton, IL U.S.A.
Madras, India / London, England

This publication made possible with the assistance of the Kern Foundation

QUEST
BOOKS

For additional information write to

Quest Books
Theosophical Publishing House
P.O. Box 270
Wheaton, IL 60187
This is a publication of The Theosophical Publishing House, a department of the Theosophical Society in America.
Sixth Printing 2018

www.questbooks.com

Library of Congress Cataloging-in-Publication Data
Eaton, Evelyn Sybil Mary, 1902–1983.
    The shaman and the medicine wheel.

    "A Quest book."
    "A Quest original"—T.P. verso.
    Includes bibliographical references.
    1. Eaton, Evelyn Sybil Mary,1902   Diaries.
2. Authors, American—20th century—Biography.
3. Healers—California—Biography.   4. Indians of North
America—Medicine.   5. Indians of North America—Religion
and mythology.   I. Title.
PS3509.A84Z47   1982   818´.5203 (B)   81-84490
ISBN 0-8356-0566-3   AACR2
ISBN 0-8356-0561-2 (pbk.)

My thanks go to the Marsden Foundation for a grant towards the expenses of research and travel, and I am also deeply indebted to those who have helped and taught me and to the Medicine Men and Women of many disciplines who have healed and strengthened me.

This book is my Give-Away to them and to "all our relatives" spread over Mother Earth. May it be a rainbow bridge between races and a signpost to fragments of the Truth.

Mahad'yuni.
(Way Shower)

Contents

Introduction

The title of this book has no reference to the author, but rather indicates the Shaman in the collective sense. I am not a Shaman. I am a Métis Medicine Woman. This is the personal log-book of a Journey, a sequel to *Snowy Earth Comes Gliding* and *I Send A Voice*, earlier accounts of experiences among Paiute, Arapaho and other tribes following traditional ways. It begins where *I Send A Voice* broke off and might be called an attempt to travel the Shamanic Journey into a realm of experience we usually believe belongs to specialists, Medicine Men and Women, Lamas, Saints, Enlightened Ones. We are not to leave it respectfully to them. It is the journey all of us will take when the time is right, and the time may be right for many who do not realize it, now.

I am, as we all are, traveling the evolutionary path to the Center and the Source of All, and like any traveler, wanting to share news and maps with others, and to learn from the experience along the way. What I have gathered so far is that we are expected to graduate from this School of Life upon our Mother Earth with the degree of perfection we can manage to achieve. The ideal set before us is perfection—"Be ye therefore perfect, as your Father in Heaven is perfect," was urged by One who never jeered or mocked or demanded the impossible. The goal will therefore

1

eventually be reached, sooner by the generous, later by the laggards. It is up to us which we choose to be.

Those on the Christian path were told, "Know ye not that we are *all* called to be saints?" The church set apart a day to consider this injunction, All Saints' Day, November 1st, and for those who cannot or will not graduate this time around, the next day is set apart, All Souls' Day, November 2nd.

Those on the Buddhic path are urged to graduate into Bodhisattvas, and in the meantime to become Gurus. A Dedication of Merit runs: "May I quickly become Guru, Lord Buddha, and lead each and every sentient being into his enlightened realm, due to these merits."

Those on the Rainbow Path of the Native American are urged to follow the example of the Great Ancestors, through purification and sacrifice (another term for "merits" perhaps) in the Sweat Lodge, in the Sun Dance, round the Medicine Wheel, and with the Pipe, that in our daily living we may help to spread the splendor of the Vision which the whole world needs. The point is we are *all* called to live up to and reveal the Light Within—to find the way no one can travel for us and to follow it to the end, the end that is likely to be a new beginning, unimaginable to us until we reach it.

PART ONE

1

PREAMBLE

From pre, before, ahead of time, and amble, to move easily. A relaxed stroll through a landscape of the mind, a preliminary survey of a subject or condition, prior to a deepening involvement.

When the Paiute Medicine Man said with stern finality: "Go and take care of the people!" I listened in dismay and deepening shock.

Many times, in Sweat Lodges, Ceremonies, Fasts and in my Pipe, I had offered myself to the Grandfathers and Those Above, asking to become a healer of little and big miseries, but in my mind this commitment was comfortably in the future, some far-off time when I would be well-trained, well-qualified and recognized, not as a Medicine Woman—I had only been going the Indian way for fifteen years and I am mostly white—but accepted as an authentic healer.

Mixed bloods have a rough time, within and without. Often there is no legal proof of genes, only word of dead mouths, our own conviction, instinctive reactions and inner certainty. We may think we know who we are. Others don't, and sometimes we don't either, except that we are born to serve as bridges between peoples and races, and who, on either side, cares deeply for a bridge, except to cross it?

🔲🔲🔲🔲

Here was the challenge, and I must rise to it, though none of the conditions I had taken for granted and assumed to be essential would be met. There would be no outward Indian authority behind me, ceremonially bestowed, and no white diploma hanging on the wall. I had the tools already given and already worked with, Pipe, Feathers, Drum, Stones, Herbs, and I had tried to align my will with the Great Will. I was not called on to "go and take care of the people" by myself. Of ourselves we can do nothing. It is the Indwelling Presence, the Creator, with the cooperation of the created, that brings all things to pass.

If Those Above accepted the awkward present I offered so rashly, so often, then we were stuck with it, with me as a channel, another pipeline between planes. It is a strange predicament for Them and for us, the tools through which They work. It comes of giving humankind free will. If, for instance, peace on earth is needed, we and "all our relatives," that is every sentient creature in the four kingdoms, mineral, vegetable, animal, human, must grow peace in our hearts, cooperate to spread peace, continue to maintain peace, agreeing together in good will. Then we shall have the peace we long for. War will never bring it.

This is so for everything that comes to pass here, a slow, frustrating way to work. Sometimes I wonder whether Wakan-Tanka is not tempted to burst forth with "Let there be PEACE!" as once with "Let there be LIGHT!" and there was Light, as there would be Peace. But it would seem that Wakan-Tanka does not intend to take back our free will, nor our imagination. What we can imagine, that we shall have. Today we are living through what collectively and individually we imagined in the past. Tomorrow we will be living through what we imagine today, for we are creative energies like the Great Energy in Whose image we are made, whether or not we realize the living force of our creations, whether or not we understand the power of our thoughts.

🔲🔲🔲🔲

I drove the long fifty-eight miles from the reservation to my then-home, shaken by the turn things seemed to be taking, wondering who "the people" were and whether "Go!" meant "Leave the Valley." Those who find their way to this desert plateau seldom want to leave it. The great granite ranges of the eastern High Sierra have a healing power. So do the creeks flowing through them, snowy-cold or mineral-hot. There are favorite mountains on either side to climb, to watch, to breathe toward, to love.

It is a strange and magic land, but it is also "Jobless Valley." Some who want to live here are forced out. Some accustomed to better living elsewhere accept sub-subsistence conditions without too much regret, in order to stay. I was one of those. I had lived for twenty years off and on, up and down the valley, not exactly jobless, since I still wrote books, but an endangered species, practically extinct, a non-pornographic, non-violent writer. Once when I described my status and occupation I was asked "Should you be at large?" and I wondered. Now it looked as though my secular life might be even more "at large."

🔲🔲🔲🔲

My neighbor's light was still on in the little cabin across the road. On an impulse I turned in there instead of into my dark driveway. I felt it would be pleasant to exchange a few cheerful words and perhaps to have a warm drink before going to what might be a sleepless night. Besides I was remembering a night years before when I had come home from a Doctoring Sweat and called on Isobel.

The living room had been empty then, except for the cat, an old and valued friend, stretched out on the sofa. I ran my hand over him and squeezed his tail in the special gesture of friendship between us. He unstretched, jumped off the sofa and purred round my feet as I made for the kitchen calling out: "Isobel! I'm glad you're still awake. Can I come in?"

The door opened. The compact little figure that always made me feel large and untidy came smiling out. Then she stopped, staring past me. I thought for a moment she was seeing the Indian Spirit Guide whom people sometimes did see behind me, but surely not Isobel, down-to-earth, practical, unimaginative Isobel. She was looking down not up. She was looking at the cat.

She said in a strange half-whisper, "What did you do to Tip?"

"Nothing."

The cat purred round our feet, tail proudly waving. He brushed past us into the kitchen. I followed nervously. My legs were turning weak and I was shivering. I began to guess what might be ahead.

"The vet's coming by presently to put him to sleep."

I stared. She stared back.

"He crossed the road and a car got him. Broke his back. The swine didn't stop. When I got there he was still alive but he couldn't move. He wasn't bleeding anywhere. He was paralyzed. He's been lying there ever since."

She backed away from me still staring. "What did you do to him?" she asked again.

Isobel was not the sort of person one could explain healing powers to, especially healing powers suddenly developed and demonstrated by a woman friend. A priest, perhaps, but even that . . . I guessed what must have happened. An extra charge had stayed in me from the Doctoring Sweat and passed into my hands, and from them into the cat, a charge strong enough to overcome paralysis, a charge strong enough not to need conscious cooperation of the channel through which it passed. If I told any of this to Isobel she would be horrified. She would think anything to do with Indian Medicine was Satanic, Devil's work, at best Witchcraft of the wrong sort, no matter how beneficent the result might be. She probably would include the cat in her fear of the Devil.

I said as nonchalantly as I could, "Aren't you going to give me some coffee? I need it."

She went to the stove then and to her turned back I was able to continue. "Well he can't have been paralyzed. He may have had a concussion. Something must have been out of whack and when I picked him up I clicked it into place again."

I knew she didn't believe me, but I thought she wouldn't probe.

"Anyhow he's all right now."

She turned to look. Tip had sprung up on the chair and was contemplating a move onto the table. Normally she would have slapped him. Now she just said "No." She poured the coffee and brought it to the table. She sat down, avoiding eye-encounter. I was beginning to shake harder. I caught myself looking at my hands.

"I think I'm catching a cold," I explained. "Have you any vitamin C?" I added, "I'm glad he's o.k. I'd have hated anything to happen to him."

We drank our coffee and talked for awhile of other things. Then I offered to run her to the phone booth to tell the vet not to come, but she said she would leave it the way it was, in case . . .

"He'll be all right," I said, as I knew he would.

I took my leave with the aspirin she gave me, having no vitamin C, and for sometime after that we were careful not to meet.

Now it was different. Years of cautious experiment had brought us to the point where I could give and she receive healing treatments, without disturbing explanations. She even sent me patients, human and animal, to treat.

Now that I was starting on a new turn of the way, it seemed appropriate to be where I first discovered and accepted full responsibility for the power surging through my hands.

We sat at the familiar table, drinking a hot drink together, but now it was not coffee, we had progressed to herbal teas.

🔲🔲🔲🔲

It might be easier for our Western-oriented minds to understand Shamanic experiences, if we relate them to other, more familiar progressions, if we remember, for instance, that Dante is considered a great Shaman, and the Shamanic journey in many ways parallels his.

Both are individual ventures into Spirit Worlds, under the guidance of supernatural beings. Dante had Virgil, Angels, Beatrice. Those who follow the Shamanic Way have Shamans, Power Animals and Grandfathers. The Eagle has a prominent part in both. Both have physical this-plane frames of reference. Both spiral through psychic realms and further, but both are firmly grounded on the earth from where they start.

Journeys start from where we are. Everything starts from where we are. Where we are is where we're supposed to be.

I was at my place on the circumference of the Medicine Wheel, a point I had reached in flashes during meditation and in dreams. Now I was freed to go further toward the Center, but before embarking on any major step of the Way, it is well to take full stock of where we are and what we know of the starting point.

What did I know of the Medicine Wheel, the journey through it, or the starting point?

I think of the Medicine Wheel as a Cosmic Blueprint, a Mandala of the Greater Medicine Wheel of the Universe, where everything created has its appropriate place, all things moving inward from the circumference to the Center.

Once we catch a glimpse of the Blueprint we find its mandalas everywhere, from massive stone circles like Stonehenge, to the child's spinning top, to the great rose windows of the Gothic Cathedrals, reflecting the Celestial Rose, beyond the limitations of time and space.

> The Will rolled onward like a Wheel
> In even motion, by the Love impelled,
> That moves the sun in Heaven and all the stars.[1]
>
>   Dante

Ezekial's vision; the zodiac; the Wheel of Life; the Serpent swallowing its tail; the Wheel of Law, Truth and Light, one of the eight emblems of good fortune in Chinese Buddhism; Navajo sand-paintings showing the creation of the world, with glyphs of the sun, earth, water, the four winds and the Four Powers ruling the Directions; these and myriad more are the mandalas of the Medicine Wheel.

Circles, rings and rounds, from the Sun, source of light and life, to the little shower ring when we cleanse our human overcoats—become reminders, shining indications, revealing ways of escape from the world of rotation and illusion to the still center of the universe.

Aristotle speaks of the "unmoved mover," Taoists speak of the "Sage," the "chosen one" invisible at the center, who moves the Wheel without moving himself. Freemasons refer to that "point within a circle, round which a Mason cannot err." Jacob Boehme, the 16th century mystic, wrote in his confessions: "The Being of God is like a Wheel, wherein many wheels are made one in another, upwards, downwards, crossways, and yet continually turn all of them together. At which indeed, when a man beholds the Wheel, he highly marvels."

These are some of the concepts daily revealed, in meditation, in observation of the worlds about us, the mineral world, Grandfather Rock with all his jewels; the plant world with all its sustenance and

---

1. Dante Alighieri, *The Vision of Dante Alighieri,* or *Hell, Purgatory and Paradise,* trans. Henry F. Cary (A. M. Dent, 1908).

beauty; the animal world with all its grace and diversity; the human world with its potentialities; the superhuman world which we are beginning to explore —these are reminders of the interdependence of the created and their relationship with the Creator, in the great wheeling dance of the universe, "whereat indeed we marvel." But marveling is not enough.

"They that live the life shall know the doctrine," one great Master said.

The Shamanic journey starts when we begin to live what we have grasped of the Great Plan.

Where do we start? Physically from where we are, however tempting it may be to wait until "the conditions are right," until we move to another place, until we get a new job, until we find more understanding, more congenial people, until . . . until . . .

The Grandfathers say "Start now." Now is all we have, all we shall ever have. Start now.

Mentally, emotionally, psychically, many of us start from where Dante started on his Shamanic journey, in the depths of a dark and gloomy wood, filled with supernatural terrors and past chaos. It is a place of great fear, "so bitter it goes nigh to death," the poet says.

"Tant' è amara che poco è piu morte."

There are several fine translations of the great poem, from Cary to Sayers, and one inspired commentary which we could take as a helpful guidebook on the journey. In it the author points out that Dante does not say "mi ritrouvai in una selva oscura," he says "per una selva oscura." It is "through the terrifying experience of the dark wood that we find the way of return to innocence," that we refind it. "The coming to consciousness is not a discovery of some new thing; it is a . . . return to that which has always been."[2]

"Oh man, remember," the Isha Upanishad admonishes, and "Remember your way out," the Grandfathers advise. Our journey is a resumption of the long way we have come, not a totally new start.

Dante resumed his journey in a dark and dreadful wood. There is a difference between a forest and a wood. A forest has space, glades and dells, sunlight filtering through the trees. Forests can be pleasant to loiter, to linger, even to live in, but for the Shamanic journey it is essential to move resolutely through a wood, and the wood is darker, more compact, full of dangerous inimical forces, wild beasts and supernatural Wendigos.

We may encounter Pan in either forest or wood but the experiences will be very different. An enchanter in a forest is one thing; a sorcerer in a wood another.

Dante looked up in his desperation. He caught a glimpse of the far-off mountain with a ray of sunshine above it and started to run forward with all his strength, but he was stopped by three ferocious beasts barring the way, a leopard, a lion and a wolf, standing in their lower selves for Lust, Pride, Greed. We know these beasts and what they symbolize and how often we encounter them and how they bar our way until we meet them shining in the Happy Hunting Grounds of Paradise.

Dante had to turn his back to the mountain and travel in the seemingly opposite direction downward into hell and through it before he could see the mountain rising ahead of him again. So it is with us.

Spiritually we start from that moment and that

---

2. Helen M. Luke, *Dark Wood to White Rose* (New York: Dover Publications, 1975).

place where we decide to re-commit ourselves to the
Journey, to re-surrender our wills to the will of the
Great Source, to enlist with finality in the Company
of Light. Sooner or later this great moment comes to
us, but it must be with finality, total commitment, we
must stick with it, or it will be only another half-
hearted attempt to take a few hesitant steps on one of
the ways leading to the Center, and away from it. We
must go forward firmly, as Dante did, or we may find
ourselves again in the dark wood. Each time this happens it gets harder to resume the journey, and
whether we go by Dante's way, on foot, or the Shamanic way "over wonderful slippery water" in a
Shadow Canoe, resumption of the journey is what
our spirits crave.

⑤⑤⑤⑤

"Sit down," the Medicine Man said, "set up a
squawk. The Grandfathers hear."

"Sit down" does not mean recline in a comfortable
armchair with a cigarette, a cup of coffee or a glass of
wine. It means sit cross-legged in a sacred manner on
our Mother Earth for a long time, many times, a pos-
ture unfamiliar to most westerners.

"Set up a squawk" does not mean make a raucous
sound of complaint. It means cry with all our being
to the Great Spirit, or, if we do not feel able to address the Source of All directly, then through an in-
termediary, a Grandfather, a Saint, a Bodhisattva,
perhaps a Power Animal or even a Stone.

Talanka Ohitika said, "Then I had a dream, and in
my dream one of these small round stones appeared
to me and told me that the Maker of All was Wakan-
Tanka and that in order to honor Him I must honor
His works in nature. The stone said that by my
search I had shown myself worthy of supernatural

help. It said that if I were curing a sick person I might ask its assistance, and that all the forces of nature would help me work a cure."

Okute or Shooter says "When a Medicine Man says that he talks with the sacred stones, it is because of all the substance in the ground these are the ones which most often appear in dreams and are able to communicate with men."

Stones have always been special companions to me. I carried them in my pockets when I was a child, and went through many shocks and crises when they were discovered and disposed of by all-powerful adults who liked pockets to be nice and clean and empty. I didn't care what they did with theirs but I wanted mine to be full of stones that I could touch and talk to through the days and sleep with at night. Even then I used special ones for healing, rubbing them on cuts and bruises before submitting to orthodox iodine and bandages.

I was a town-bred, town-raised child, whose parents traveled a great deal so that I had no roots in any one town or even continent. I was educated first by governesses, French, German, English, then in Canadian and English boarding schools. None of these educational authorities had much knowledge of what they called "the Redskins," sometimes "the savages." I don't believe it crossed their minds that there could be anything worth knowing about Indians. As for my Algonquin heritage, no one mentioned it.

Later, estranged and severed from my family, I lived and worked in Paris through the depression and until the rise of Hitler, when I took refuge, first in England, then in Canada, and finally in the United States. This town-life of poverty, stress and displacement made it difficult to keep in good relationship with Mother Earth or even to find right stones. My childhood knowledge went latent from my conscious life for many years.

It was decades, in fact, before I became re-aware of innate kinship with Grandfather Rock and the mineral world. I was not fully awake to the interdependence of sentient beings on different levels of existence, when I received an ancient healing stone from a Medicine Man in Wyoming at the time of my first fast. I treasured the stone for a long time without knowing how to use it or even that it should be used, until it became impatient to be healing and told me so in dreams. Since then I have been given other healing stones, including different forms of crystals, but this first-come stone of sacred red rock remains my fundamental power-stone.

It was when I began to give thanks for the special rocks in the Sweat Lodges that I began to see their faces. Later as I traveled with companions to seminars and other Grandfather-directed missions, reflections of mineral "relatives" emerged on rock surfaces at significant moments, appearing and disappearing as we watched, leaving us with a sense of renewed strength and blessing.

This experience will come to those, but only those, who do not misuse the mineral world, who recognize and respect Life in every sentient atom, who understand that rocks are sentient too, a truth now cautiously admitted by some "scientific minds," since recent experiments have shown that rocks can be sick and recover from sickness. The truth goes deeper, but even this much concession toward the realities known to travelers of traditional ways for thousands of years and taken for granted by them, is a big step forward. It is a step the human race must surely take if we are to continue in existence here, in kinship with the Earth and our relatives upon Her.

When we visit rock drawings, or study illustrations of them and other universal symbols of the Wheel, or talk with friends about the experiences which come to us on the spiral journey, we wonder how Indian and non-Indian people, all interested people, Métis,[3] can best use the knowledge filtered through to us from so many ancient sources.

The more we meditate on the Medicine Wheel and the Greater Wheel Above, the Cosmic Wheel, relating these to circles, spheres, mandalas of other traditions, the deeper grows our realization of the oneness of the myriad paths leading to the Center.

As we discover our right places and see the appropriate place of everyone and everything upon the Wheel, the less we are troubled with intolerance, that densest barrier to spiritual growth. When we see someone traveling a path which seems the opposite to ours, we no longer make the mistake of crying out: "No! No! You must come all the way round the circumference to where I am and go in exactly as I go. I have the only truth. Mine is the only way!"

As the Medicine Wheel becomes the background of our lives, the foreground too, we come to know that there are countless ways to the Center, as many ways as there are wayfarers. The wise of old, the Chinese, the Tibetan sage, the Indian following the traditional way, never made the mistake of missionizing. They had no problems with their own intolerance, though plenty with other people's intolerance to-

---

3. Métis. See End Notes.

wards them. As one elder said to me, "if my brother stands upon his head and believes he is worshipping Wakan-Tanka, then he is worshipping Wakan-Tanka. I respect that. I may try it myself to make him feel good about his way."

Throughout the ages man's inhumanity to man, enforced conformity under torture and threats of eternal fire have never been efficacious ways of converting souls to this or that man-made doctrine. It is not a lasting way of attracting people to change their convictions. There have always been fanatics, power-mad prelates and dictators, convinced that their way to "salvation" is the only way, though the Sources to which they pay official lip service teach otherwise.

Jesus said, "Let your light so shine before men that they may see your good works and glorify your Father Which is in Heaven."

It is the light, the aura of the illumined, as they go about their daily living, that attracts us to the Source their light reflects.

We revere Dante for his great wheeling circle of the Celestial Rose, the center of which, the circle of light, is the light of the Great Spirit's Glory. We should meditate on this part of his Medicine Wheel, more than on the lurid descriptions of Hell students pore over at school. Unfortunately of the three divisions of the poem, the first one, the Inferno is often the only one offered in the curriculum. Without the other two it loses most of Dante's message. It becomes a rather violent, almost sordid story, instead of one necessary and supportive part of the redemptive whole.

We should not "give any mind to," i.e., support with any of our energies, false concepts of the past, or of the present, unnecessary hells we make for ourselves through ignorance and arrogance. Hell was originally only another name for the underworld, the lower strata of the astral plane. Then power-crazed, perverted minds twisted it to mean a place of eternal punishment where souls must suffer agonizing tortures forever for breaking misunderstood, man-invented laws.

Not so long ago it was an accepted doctrine of the Christian Church that babies dying before they were baptized would burn forever in the fires of Hell. Anguished parents were obliged to believe this horror in the name of the loving Father. If they were unable to find a priest in time, or to persuade him to come, if they were too poor to pay, or at odds with the Church and so denied the sacraments, including the sacrament of Baptism, they suffered psychological wounds, mental and emotional breakdowns, lasting sometimes all their lives.

"The common people," wiser, often more compassionate and nearer to the truth than self-appointed "spiritual" leaders, took to baptizing dying babies whenever and however they could. Some anxious parents baptized every new-born baby, well or ill. The practice became so widespread that the Church eventually had to accept it, and "Provisional Baptism" was sanctioned, safeguarded by rules, and always provided that it was repeated by a priest, if the child lived. If the child died there remained a doubt whether hasty baptism by a lay person would be enough to save it from eternal torture.

Meanwhile the majority of babies on the earth didn't stand a chance, nor their parents. The bulk of humankind was doomed to Hell forever, because there was only one narrow, priest-controlled way of escape, through one minority religion. It seems incredible, but people did believe it, and other equally monstrous "articles of the true Faith."

Dante took one live man through Hell, and that was a daring innovation, but even he, great visionary Shaman that he was, did not go openly against the Church's official teachings. He lifted the level of the meaning of Hell by suggesting that sin itself, the condition of being in sin, sin embraced by obdurate souls, was the real Hell. We can accept that, from our own experience and understanding of conditions we have earned and reaped. It is the "no escape" that rings untrue. We speak with instinctive wisdom when we say someone "has been through Hell," or "So-and-so is going through Hell." It is through. Nothing is static, nothing blocked "forever."

Dante gives some indications in his Log-book that he represents humanity, that he is Everyman. By implication, if one man passed through hell and emerged from it, others can. True he was summoned, guided and vouched for by supernatural beings, sent from Those Above. So are we protected and attended on our way by Guides.

Dante would have appreciated the anonymous mystic who settled the subject of Hell to his own satisfaction and the relief of co-religionists by saying: "We must accept that Hell exists, but we are free to believe that there is no one in it."

Nowadays we have sources Dante never heard of, e.g., The Tibetan Book of the Dead with its detailed, almost mapped and charted, guided journeys through the Bardo, the Underworld, for which Hell was originally another name. We have the Egyptian Book of the Dead. We have visions and accounts of the Happy Hunting Ground.

The concept of Hell never troubled natives following the traditional way. It was never a doctrine of the wise. There are fanatics in the world today, convinced that their way to "salvation" is the only way, and ready to force it on the rest of us by torture if necessary. Their definition of salvation is as distorted as their definition of Hell. It is their problem, not ours. Ours is to make sure there is no intolerance, in us, and no resentment even of fanatics.

Speaking of the Happy Hunting Ground the elder said, "No trouble There. There They all get along good. Don't make a bit of difference what name we use, Wakan-Tanka, Great-Grandfather, God, Creator, all the same. What we have to do here, we have to live good. Be kind. Love our relatives, animals, rocks, plants, respect our Mother Earth. Take care of her." He thought for awhile, then he said gravely: "What we don't do here we have to do There. Then it's harder. Better learn all we can now, work at it now, then when we get up There They can teach us new things."

🔲🔲🔲🔲

When I was a child in England I was introduced to one of the great Mandalas of the European Hemisphere. I was taken to Winchester to see King Arthur's Table Round hanging on one of the cathedral walls. It was a familiar sight. King Arthur and his Knights were popular among Edwardian parents and educators, constantly invoked as models for children to live by. Lord Tennyson's *Idylls of the King* was read aloud, memorized, reproduced in plays for children, and generally was a large part of nursery and schoolroom life. There were pictures of the Holy Grail above our beds and about our ways, ranging from a puzzled dove to a sort of misty shawl, a "comforter" like those the grown-ups put around their shoulders on chilly evenings. The Holy Ghost was a comforter too. They said so in Church. The two Holies were probably related, maybe even twins, I thought.

Later came a period of backlash and reaction against Victorianism. Romance and chivalry and Tennyson were out. Fairy tales were taken away. I know a college professor, head of an English department who wrote a textbook on the Arthurian Legends which is still widely in use. He left out the Holy Grail. It was, he said, "irrelevant." But the Quest of the Holy Grail is the English Shamanic Journey, and the Table Round its mandala. The Knights sat under their banners and shields, representing moral qualities, wisdom, justice, courage, strength, etc. Indians also have shields with devices on them representing qualities sacred to the shield-bearers.

I know of a group of assorted ages and races, who are using an old wagon wheel for meditation. It is placed on the ground, appropriately painted in the four significant colors, with ancient symbols designed on the circumference. The person seated at the segment representing serenity tries to live that quality, to be serene in all the varying tests of life, what one mystic has called "the daily startle of the world," so that the group as a whole can depend upon the serenity of the circle being steadily maintained, safe in the keeping of that person. The one sitting in the seat of truth lives truth in all the facets of personal life, so that at the meeting of the group, and in between meetings, the truth of the circle stays steady and firm. The one representing courage shows courage in the events of daily life, so that the courage of the group is steadily maintained. All these qualities can be called upon by any member of the group in need of them. From time to time the wheel is turned, so that the qualities are represented by different people.

Old wagon wheels are not always handy. Some of us live in cities. If for any reason we cannot lay out our Medicine Wheel of stones, it is probably still possible to spread a cloth or a canvas or a piece of paper on the floor, with a circle on it, radii going toward the hub, and to seat ourselves in meditation round it. If none of this is possible we can seat ourselves mentally at any point of the Medicine Wheel, alone, and offer to represent for that day or that week or that month, the quality of that part of the Wheel. Moving toward the center, along any of the paths or radii, even if we have to do it only in our minds—"my mind to me a kingdom is"—we grow in understanding of one of the paths to the Great Spirit. There is really no excuse for not practicing what we have learned about the way.

One of the attractive things about this exercise in understanding ourselves and our places on the Wheel is its perfect democracy. The round table ensured no head or foot, no above or below the salt, every member seated there was equal to every other member. So also the Indian circle round the fire, in the Sweats and Ceremonies, is a perfect democracy. However young, however old, every member of the tribe has his or her place; no more no less than another's. I have sat between a ninety year old man and a seven month old girl. Each received the same attention from the Medicine Man.

As an exercise toward growth we can also adopt the right approach to our Mother the Earth and all who share her with us, the rocks, the vegetation, our kindred the animals, the birds, an approach without fear, with respect and love, even towards a snake. If a rattlesnake, for example, waits across our path, we should not hurl at him our hatred, our terror, our intent to kill, but send out a vibration of love, or if we can't quite manage that, conditioned as we are by our false education and rigid cultural background, at least of interest and admiration, with perhaps a polite request that he move on somewhere else, although he has the same right to be on our Mother Earth and in that particular place as we have.

I have encountered rattlers and copperheads and watched them peacefully depart when I have asked them to. Once a child who was with me jumped back with a scream on seeing a large snake, a harmless one this time, but she had come upon it suddenly. She said, "I'm scared of snakes, but if you leave them alone, they'll leave you alone." I agreed, and told her how we might go further in our reactions and change our feelings towards a snake.

We can encourage in ourselves and in our children a right attitude towards ecology. We can remind ourselves that the well bred Indian, or any aware person, for that matter, should be able to pass through the world without leaving a trace of any physical presence, without litter, without carving our initials on trees and rocks, hurting and insulting them, without changing anything, walking carefully, gently on our Mother Earth, leaving everything the way we find it, unless there is something out of place like a beer can which we should take away.

We can be aware of many signs and tokens the Grandfathers show us to remind us of the Great Spirit. We could look more closely at the flowers, for example, their shapes and colors, considering what these mean. The four petalled wild rose might remind us of the Four Directions, the Four Old Men, the Four Great Powers, the Cross. Its pink color is the color of love, so that we have the cross of sacrifice and the rose of love in this one symbol. Other flowers, among them the sunflower, obviously, represent the sun and all that the sun stands for, Light and Life-Bearer, reminder of the Source of all.

Mostly we can change our attitude toward the people and situations in our daily living. We can adopt the blessed relief of living in the *now,* responsible only for the short interval of the passing hours, flowing with the flow, endeavoring to remain in harmony with the Great Spirit and to be open channels for That One's blessing to the world. We do not have to think about the past nor to anticipate the future. We are in the *now,* the moment that we have, the immortal now, which is all that anyone can have. As hour by hour, day by day, we change our attitudes towards our surroundings, a corresponding change will take place in ourselves.

▣▣▣▣

These are the suggestions, the hints that come to me in answer to the questions I receive from other travelers, an abc for those setting forth to find what some have known for many centuries, what we too have dimly known and often missed, needed then and are needing now. "They that live the life shall know the doctrine." It is not the other way about. Through the ages candidates for the true Mysteries were taught to "do in symbol what hereafter they would do in fact," and to start from where they found themselves on the paths that they were taking.

If we begin, slowly, gently, to put the new attitudes, our new orientation, into practice, "aujourd-'hui plus qu'hier et biens moins que demain," (Today more than yesterday and much less than tomorrow.) as the poet Verhaeren said that he advanced in love, we will find wisdom, strength and certitude unfolding within us.

As an anonymous mystic testified, "If therefore ye are intent upon wisdom a lamp will not be wanting and a shepherd will not fail, and a fountain will not dry up." Another reported "and the Voice went forth throughout the world . . . and each one heard it according to his capacity . . . the Voice was to each one as each had power to receive it."

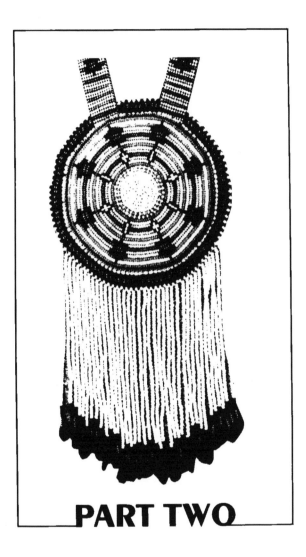

PART TWO

2

When the time is right to harmonize ourselves with
Grandfather Rock and the mineral world before laying out a Medicine Wheel, those, who are able to,
might go on a pilgrimage, make a vision quest, take a
holy day (holiday not vacation, which comes from the
root word meaning emptiness) to some of the awesome power centers of the world, Stonehenge, Ave-
bury, Karnak, the Grand Canyon, Bryce Canyon,
Death Valley, places where the veils are thin between
planes and forces, where the three-dimensional and
the more-dimensional sometimes meet and merge.

It is not necessary to make the journey physically,
though millions do, mostly on "vacation," the limited experiences of shallow approaches to the wonders of the world. But nowadays there are superb
photographs of most of the breakthrough places still
undefiled upon our Mother Earth. We might make
mini-pilgrimages to the public libraries, stock up on
books and magazines to use as meditation warm-ups;
and "fly with the wild geese."

Travel in imagination has some advantages. We
can choose to be alone in the Grand Canyon, alone
on the top of Mount Shasta, alone in Monument Valley, or we may choose companions, alter egos, to en-

31

rich the experience. We can create the conditions we relate to best—sunrise, sunset, rising moon, spring, summer, fall, winter.

Of course it is good to travel in the imagination *and* to have physical access to places of silence and solitude charged with spiritual force and transformative power. I live near some of the oldest and most fantastic rock formations in the world, huge boulders, crest upon crest of primeval, impressionistic shapes, in the foothills below the High Sierra near Mount Whitney. I drove a sculptor through them once. After the first mile he wept. "What's the use?" he whispered, "It's all been done!" He meant by the Supreme Artist. He was right.

Those who follow Dante's Shamanic journey, those who relate to Tolkien and take him for their Virgil, would feel at home here, not cosily at home, not all at ease, because it can be frightening. To me it is more awe-inspiring than the famous Dante's Lookout in nearby Death Valley, to me it has stronger vibrations and more evidence of the presence of Grandfather Rock.

Some years ago, between 1965 and 1968, a small private foundation to which I belong, sponsored concerts of classical music in this setting, for three weekends each summer. People sat on the ground between the rocks, watching the sunset and the moon rise over a landscape too stupendous to be quite terrestrial. Without the presence of anything artificial, (a shell, a microphone, electricity, a generator, benches, chairs,) the chosen circle of great rocks provided perfect acoustics, undistorted pure dynamics. A harpsichord, a symphony orchestra, the softest whisper, the loudest choral ensemble, were heard and experienced as if for the first time by astonished people suddenly aware of vaster sounds beyond ears' reach.

On the night that Harihar Rao and his wife played Hindu music there, Aim Morhardt[1] wrote:

The small amphitheater, set well apart from any distractions, is framed, like a far more ancient Stonehenge, with its incredible granite monoliths. Those of us who were there early watched evening fall over the Sierra crest. A fingernail moon and its attendant evening star stayed briefly with us as the sky darkened, only to drop, before darkness, behind the dragon crest of Whitney. One by one the druid lights were lit, each in its natural rock cavity. The absolute serenity of the quiet warm night gathered us into its magic. The Polynesian lamps of the stage were lit, and with a first light whisper of wind the performance began. Lacking the stage it might well have been two thousand years ago in the Khyber Pass. As an experience in today's world it was profoundly affecting.

It was, as 95 percent of classical Hindu music is, unwritten patterns handed down through generations from teacher to gifted student, basing itself only briefly on the basic framework of the particular raga used, and from that point going off into an improvisational theme and variations on an enormously extended melodic line. It was a quiet tale at first, but as it progressed it kept on adding more and more intricate configurations. Keeping pace with it, the wind also came, whispering down around the rocks, blowing the stage lights into trails of flame which became in turn like some occult choreography sent by the djinns of our own ancient hills to keep him company. Variation piled on variation against the groundbeat of the C

---

1. Aim Morhardt. See End Notes.

sharp tonic, endlessly repeated, and the susurra-
tion of the 13 'sympathetic' unplayed strings
which are part of the instrument. And then, with a
last gentle statement, it was over, and the audience came back to reality.

Or did we *leave* reality? As a 'sympathetic unplayed string' I think we did.

One unforgettable night Iren Marik and John Ranck[2]
who premiered Messiaen's *Vision des Septs Amens*
for two pianos, in New York in 1963, played it again
in the attentive desert under the wide sky, while
Grandfather Rock's massive formations seemed to
lean forward as they listened.

These seven great amens are a helpful preparation
for meditation on the Cosmic Medicine Wheel. *Amen*,
the composer says, has four different meanings:
1) *Amen*—Let it be so—(So mote it be)—the Act of creation. 2) *Amen*—I yield. I accept. Thy will be done.
3) *Amen*—The wish, the desire that this be so—that
You (God) give Yourself to me and I to you. 4) *Amen*
—It *is* so, all is eternally decided—consummated in
Paradise.

"By joining the lives of the creatures who say
Amen because they exist, I have tried to express the
infinite variety of riches of the Amen in seven Musi-
cal Visions."

Dante was a "faithful son of the church," a mystic,
working within the framework of medieval beliefs,
though often transcending them. Messiaen also uses
Christian images, and like Dante outsoars them,
opening doors to wider consciousness. There is no
conflict between these visions of the Cosmic Blueprint, and the Shamanic vision of the entrance to Shipapo, all are ignited from the central Source of Light.

---

2. Iren Marik, John Ranck. See End Notes.

Dante's journey is translated into the poetry of a towering genius. Messiaen's into contemporary music, the Shamanic into the practice of a close relationship with Those Above and Those Below, and Those Around us, particularly of our Mother Earth. It is the way of practical hour-to-hour involvement. "The truth is not just something theoretical—it is something that *works*."

Messiaen supplied some program notes for the premiere of his composition:

1. *The Amen of the Creation.*

Amen, let it be so. God said "Let there be Light and there was Light." (Genesis) The whole piece is a crescendo. It starts with the most complete pianissimo in the mystery of the first nebula which already contains the power of the Light . . . all the bells which tremble in this Light . . . the Light which is LIFE.

2. *The Amen of the Stars and the planet of the rings.*

A brutal and savage dance. The stars, the suns, and Saturn, the planet with the multicolored rings, are turning violently. God calls them and they say, "Amen, here we are." (Book of Baruch) All these movements mixed together evoke the life of the planets and of the astonishing rainbow which colors the turning rings of Saturn.

3. *The Amen of the Agony of Jesus.*

Jesus suffers and weeps. "My Father, if this cup may not pass from me without my drinking it, may Thy will be done and not my will" (Gospel according to St. Matthew). He accepts. Let Thy will be done. Amen. Jesus is alone in the Garden of the Olive Trees (Gethsemane) facing his Agony. A cry, rhythmic and expressive grouping, a tormented lament in four notes. Then return to the theme of the Creation. A great silence, cut with a few pulsations, evokes the sufferings of this hour . . . inexpressible suffering, which is revealed only slightly by the sweat of blood.

4. *The Amen of Desire.*

Two themes of desire. The first, slow, ecstatic, the craving for a deep tenderness . . . already the calm perfume of Paradise. The second extremely passionate . . . the soul is drawn by a terrible love which expresses itself in a fleshly fashion (the Song of Songs) but there is nothing here of the flesh, only a paroxysm of the thirst of LOVE. Then a large and peaceful ending on the first theme. The two principal voices seem to melt into one another, and nothing is left but the harmonious silence of heaven,

5. *The Amen of the Angels, the Saints, and the Song of Birds.*

Song of the purity of the Saints: Amen. The birds sing urgently: Amen. Angels prostrate themselves before the Throne: Amen. (Revelations of St. John.)

First the song of the Angels and the Saints, stripped to essentials, very pure. Then the middle part, or the song of the birds, giving opportunity for brilliant piano composition.

These are the real songs of nightingales, thrushes, blackbirds, and finches, and their noisy and happy mixture. Return to the song of the saints. Brief coda on the birds.

6. *The Amen of the Judgment.*

Three notes as cold as the judgment bell. In truth I say unto you, Amen. "You cursed ones retire from me!" (Gospel according to St. Matthew.) The damned are relegated to their condition (of being damned). The piece is intentionally hard and short.

7. *The Amen of the Consummation.*

The Consummation is Heaven: The life of the Blessed in showers of light. "From brightness to brightness" (Proverbs) Amen. The second piano takes up the theme again in the chords of Creation, and derives from it a long chorus of glory. The first piano surrounds the second (octaves extremely heavy and extremely sharp together), with an incessant shower of harmonies and brilliant rhythms, sparkling, in rhythmic canons more and more tightly constructed . . . the precious jewels of the Apocalypse which ring, clash, dance, color and perfume the Light of Life.

Ten years after the last note of the last concert died away among the rocks I began taking groups of "the people" to this ancient, sacred, highly charged region, for fasts, vision quests, pipe ceremonies and rituals around the Medicine Wheel.

On June 13th, 1980, my log book says:

We started tonight on a vision quest. We went first for a purifying swim in Manzanar. It was very full and we had it to ourselves. Icy cold, refreshing. Then to the place behind and above where the concerts used to be. Here we laid out a big Medicine Wheel. We danced, we sang four songs, we smoked our pipes, each in place on the circumference. Meditation began as darkness fell and the stars appeared, luminously brilliant in these wide clear skies.

After a long silence of contemplation P. played the flute, K. the drum, C. and J. spoke softly, E. sang and sang. The others attended them in silence. Then we "traveled" along the stones in front of us into the Center, and after a timeless time returned to the circumference, to lie in our bags and blankets, feet toward the Hub, watching the Cosmic Wheel turn above us. There were two Medicine Wheels, the one laid out below, the one made manifest above.

When the first glimmer of the pre-dawn light outlined the ring of worshipping boulders, we rose to greet the sun. In this reminiscent setting the song of the ancient Egyptian greeting returned to our minds —"Hail Ra in Thy rising!" Then we smoked the morning Pipe to Wakan-Tanka, dismantled the Medicine Wheel, left an offering among the rocks, and proceeded to another place some miles away to make ready individual shelters for a two-night fast, part of "taking care of the people" the Grandfathers were sending to us in growing numbers.

The Grandfathers and Grandmothers need no definition for Turtle Islanders and those following the traditional native American ways. For those to whom these ancient wide-spread ways seem new and strange, the Grandfathers are the High Consistory of Those Above, Representatives and Agents of Wakan-Tanka, Attributes of the Great Spirit, Archangels, Perfected Beings, Saints, Bodhisattvas, the Hierarchy of Healers. They answer to these and many other appelations, none of which contains the only truth. There is no last word about the Grandfathers and Grandmothers. However we think of Them, however we address Them, we have one certainty. They always hear, They always answer. Sometimes Their answers surprise or disconcert us. They have been called the Cosmic Humorists. Humor is a healing power. The lack of it usually denotes the presence of someone or something from our opposite Outfit, the Army of Darkness. Kindly humor is holy, making people laugh is excellent Medicine. We do not practice it enough. We allow the prophets of doom and gloom to darken our days, forgetting that as Donne pointed out, "God is not a dampe," nor does the Great Spirit smile on those who dampen others and take the stars out of happy eyes.

The Medicine Wheel of the Mineral World

Collecting stones is the first step toward setting up the Wheel. Logically, perhaps, where we are going to put it should come first, but there can be no general rule for this. It varies from person to person, day to day and changing circumstances. We can be delayed or even lost in searching for the perfect place and the right conditions. It is best in this as in other stages of the journey to work from where we are and what we have around us since that is where the needs are and why we are there to meet them. With ingenuity and patience right solutions will be found, right answers to the where and when.

So first we collect the stones. They should come from different places, bringing the influence, the

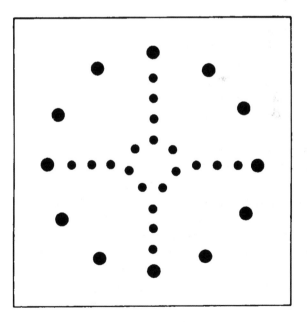

Diagram of the Medicine Wheel.

powers and vibrations of those places with them. This is part of their contribution to the work they are to share in, work which will help them to advance in their evolution as it will help us to advance in ours.

Specifically where do we find them? If we live in any of the big coastal cities we probably have access to beaches. There we can find stones of different shapes and colors, smoothed by the power of the sea and containing some of her vibrations. These are excellent for work on the Wheel.

If we live inland and can get into the countryside, stones from riverbeds, streams, the roots of trees, along banks, or in any quiet place we find them, are good and can be used in the Wheel. When a stone suddenly "speaks" from such a place, stands out to attract our attention, we should welcome it as a willing candidate for the work.

When we find a suitable stone, or when we take any stone for any reason, we should leave an offering in its place. First we must explain to Grandfather Rock why we want to take this stone from its living space, and then to the stone itself why we are taking it, for what unselfish purpose. Then we put out the offering, tobacco, or corn pollen, or some other token of love and respect, expressing our thanks to Grandfather Rock as the Guardian of the Mineral World and the Representative of Mother Earth. Then we bring the stone home and treat it rightly with affectionate respect, and finally we lay it out to do its work with the other stones on the Wheel.

If we live in such a place and such a way that we cannot get to the sea or countryside even for a "vacation" we might ask more fortunate friends to bring us stones from their travels, explaining the kinds we need, and if they have hearing ears, why the stones are needed. Perhaps these friends will later join us round the Wheel.

As a last resort there are rock shops where we can buy stones, setting them free from debasing bondage to commercialism, a form of slavery.

The size of the stones we need will vary with our circumstances. If we live in an apartment we will look for small stones, pebbles, to use on a table or part of the living-room floor, if we have a garden or backyard, for larger stones. The main thing is to treat them rightly from the moment that we meet them, remembering that they are sentient, that Grandfather Rock stands behind them and the mineral nature spirits with them and that we need their cooperation as they need ours.

The more we know of the wonders of the mineral kingdom the better, but it does not matter if we don't know much about geology or so-called "scientific" facts about minerals. The important thing is our personal relationship with the rocks we take into our force fields, our intuitive awareness of their place and ours on the Medicine Wheel.

The Chinese painters of the T'ang Dynasty and on through the seventeenth century have helpful advice for us. Kio Jo-hsu said:

> He who is learning to paint must first still his heart, thus to clarify his understanding and increase his wisdom. In stilling the heart an individual can become one with the elements of nature, the great creative forces of Tao. Stilling the heart beautifully expresses the quietness necessary for creative results, an inner quietness related to the silence of Tao and its processes. To clarify understanding and increase wisdom means a contemplative attention to all of nature's changes in order

gradually to gain a sense of the permanent and significant. In estimating people, their quality of spirit (ch'i) is as basic as the way they are formed; and so it is with rocks, which are the framework of the heavens and of earth and also have ch'i. That is the reason rocks are sometimes spoken of as "roots of the clouds." To depict rocks with ch'i, one must seek it beyond the material and in the intangible.

Lu Ch'ai said that the main thing in painting rocks was that they should be alive.

Large and small rocks mingle and are related like the pieces on a chessboard. Small rocks near water are like children gathered around with arms outstretched toward the mother rock. On a mountain it is the large rock, the elder, that seems to reach out and gather the children about him. There is kinship among rocks. The analogy of kinship implies the relatedness and an ideal of harmony in all of nature, illustrating also the underlying ritual and reverent attitude. The grouping of rocks near water and on a mountain suggest also the idea of Yin (Feminine and Water Principle) and Yang (Masculine and Mountain Principle).

Aspasia Voulis, a modern "structurist-painter," teacher to a privileged few, begins her classes by telling her students to look at a rock (we seldom look at anything with full attention) familiarize ourselves with it, and then get inside the rock until we can feel the ground beneath us as the rock feels it. Then we may take charcoal and draw the mass of the rock, only the mass, and when we have that, start the actual drawing of the rock.

We may not be going to draw the rocks we use in the Medicine Wheel, although it would not hurt to try, but the approach of ancient Chinese and modern artists will help us to create the right relationship from the start. "If the form of the rock is not clear in one's heart and from there to the finger tips the picture can never be completely realized."[3] (For "picture" read "relationship.")

Before laying out the Wheel we should remove shoes, glasses, watches, irrelevant jewelry, etc. Shoes, because we are about to set apart some holy ground, and also that we may come in closer contact with Mother Earth; glasses because we are not going to use artificial eyesight, but a more perfect, inner vision; watches because we are not going to be bound by man-created watch-time, we are going into timeless space; jewelry or other unnecessaries because we do not want to be burdened with any kind of habitual fetter.

The important thing is to remove these vibrations from our hearts and minds as we remove them symbolically from our human envelopes. We need not be fanatic. If, for instance, it would deeply disturb us to remove our glasses, then let us wear them, and still make the inward leap to clearer vision, forgetting the limitations of our physical envelopes.

The next step is to purify and consecrate ourselves and everything we intend to use by "smudging" them. Smudging means burning sage, sweet grass, cedar, or other pure incense in a round container, dispensing the rising smoke in a ritual way. Sage growing wild on the mountains and deserts is most generally used in the West, but there is an appropriate herb available regionally if we search for it, or if we live in the wilds of a great city, we can send away

---

3. Mai-Mai Sze, The Way of Chinese Painting (New York: Random House, 1959).

for a supply. If we use commercial incense, it must not be made with musk, which lowers and thickens the vibrations.

There are precedents for smudging (the use of incense) in all the major religions.

> He sacrificed also and burned incense in the high places; and on the hills, and under every given tree.
>
> > 11 Chronicles, 28.4.

> From the rising up of the sun unto the going down of the same the Lord's Name shall be magnified; and in every place incense shall be offered unto His Name and a pure offering.
>
> > Psalms.

> As this incense rises before Thee so let our prayer be set forth in Thy sight. Let Thy holy Angels encompass Thy people and breathe forth upon them the spirit of Thy blessing.
>
> > Liberal Catholic Church Liturgy.

> Smoke rises from the sweet grass. Medicine Elk purifies his hands in the incense four times. He kneels and bathes his head and body in the sweet grass incense. He moves around the smoking incense on his knees, symbolically facing each of the four directions and the center of the universe as he turns. Now Medicine Elk has been purified for his work.
>
> > *Sweet Medicine.* Peter J. Powell.

These are not interesting descriptions of rituals performed long ago, or perhaps nowadays, but for others to use. They are procedures to be taken literally and carefully followed by those aspiring to the Shamanic journey.

The first is for outdoor rituals; the second says significantly "in *every* place." People following the traditional ways observe this better than the average non-Indian. Their homes, their meals, their trucks, their tools, the work they are doing, are "smudged" constantly, also gifts given and received, sacred objects, all their *medicine*, which means their hourly ways of living. The third is to invite unseen Presences, Healers and Helpers, Power Animals, Grandfathers and Grandmothers, Devas, Angels, to join in the work and give their blessings. The fourth describes the preparation of a great Shaman for a special operation. We need not follow this exactly, but if we choose to, it is helpful and complete.

🔲🔲🔲🔲

It may be that, searching for stones for a Medicine Wheel, we find a healing stone. Healing stones come in many kinds and forms. The most usual is round, domed on the top, flat beneath. It should fit into the palm of the hand, curved side uppermost, flat side ready to be passed over the etheric body of a patient, or object needing healing. There are other shapes and forms and colors. Crystals, for example, come in myriad forms for myriad uses; but the rounded, turtle-backed stones are those we are most likely to encounter first.

Healing stones are very advanced in mineral evolution. They are highly sensitive, deeply aware of our needs, generously ready to help their relatives, but sometimes they are over-generous, sometimes we draw on them to the edge of exploitation. They forgive us, knowing we go wrong from ignorance, but ignorance is no excuse. Cosmic laws take no account of it. We should remember that stones, like us, can be tired to the point of exhaustion, and if we still exact more work from them and they still generously cooperate, they may fall seriously ill, they may even lose their ch'i and "die" from this misuse.

It is essential to remember that all living creatures, especially those in healing work, need spiritual and physical refueling. From time to time we should take healing stones to the sea or to running streams and wash them well, asking the elementals of the water to replenish them with strength and well-being.

Crystals, especially, are prone to depletion through overuse. When they weaken, it helps to bury them in a container of pure seasalt, obtainable at Health food and other with-it stores. We should cover them completely and leave them to rest for a period of days or weeks. Then we should bathe them in sea or stream and wrap them in silk. Crystals should be kept in silk. Separate silken bags are best.

How many stones are needed to lay out a Medicine Wheel? The diagram we are using shows thirty-two. Sometimes we may need more, but let us start with these.

When the Wheel is laid out as in the diagram, it must be consecrated for the work to be done.

One good method to consecrate something is to sit cross-legged on the ground, facing East, then ask the elementals of fire to light the sage and keep it burning. Do not blow out the match. Breath is to enkindle, not to extinguish. Shake it out and thank the elementals for their help. Take the smoke from the smouldering sage four times in cupped hands, passing it over head, face and down the body. Then smudge the objects to be blessed, passing them sunwise across the smoke, from east to west, from south to north, from west to east, from north to south in the form of a cross, which brings them to the interested attention of the Four Great Powers who rule the Four Directions. Then raise them to Grandfather Sky and lower them to Mother Earth, thus completing the Six Directions.

To consecrate a Medicine Wheel or other space or boundary, first smudge yourself, facing East; then move barefoot from point to designated point, always sunwise. It is not necessary to smudge the thirty-two stones individually. When they are all in place, take the sage and waft the smoke round the circumference, up the four cross lines, round the inner circle and finally to the center stone, with special care, for it represents Wakan-Tanka, Great Energy, Source of all.

With the Wheel laid out, blessed and ready, and ourselves ready also, we take our places round it. There are different ways of doing this. Sun Bear, Métis Medicine Chief of the Bear Medicine Tribe, places his people astrologically around the circumference. According to the Bears, "the moon, or month during which you were born determines your starting place on the Medicine Wheel and your beginning totem in the mineral, plant and animal kingdoms."[4]

The starting place is only a starting place. His people stand for the ceremony, then pass around the Wheel, with the responsibility of learning about the different moons, totems, plants and elements through which they pass. Sun Bear and his co-author Wabun tell us in their inspired book *The Medicine Wheel, Earth Astrology:*

> The essence of the Medicine Wheel is movement and change. Through this knowledge people attempt to allow themselves as much room for change in any one life as they can handle. They

---

4. Sun Bear and Wabun, *The Medicine Wheel, Earth Astrology* (Englewood Cliffs: Prentice Hall, 1980).

wish to progress around the Wheel and experience as many manifestations of human nature as
possible. They know that they contain all of these
manifestations within themselves, but they have
to place themselves in various positions and experiences in order to feel them.[5]

Finding our places by whatever method, Sun
Bear's or another, seemingly more haphazard, but always as the Grandfathers and the Deva of the Wheel
direct, we gather in our circle around the circumference. We do not stand, nor circumambulate, for this
exercise. We sit cross-legged behind the stones on
the outer edge, placing ourselves symbolically in
those "various positions and experiences" Sun Bear
speaks of, to enter this meditation. Meditation,
though possible in any position, seems to come more
naturally, or rather we come more naturally to meditation, when we are seated in a sacred manner than
when we stand.

Depending on the number of people present each
should be behind a stone on the circumference. Four
will be behind the four pathways from the Four Directions. Those with only one stone in front of them
should create three more stones to build their pathways toward the circle of seven stones round the
Center. Check with the diagram. By "create" I mean
use the strongest tool we have, the imagination.

If you are working the Wheel alone, you may sit before any of the four pathways to the Four Directions.
Generally one sits in the west, facing east.

The Medicine Wheel is a summary of all that is,
containing everything known and unknown in the

---

5. Ibid.

universe, therefore the stones can be taken to represent anything, everything, nations, problems, people, qualities.

The ability to relate to it with ease and reassurance through much practice, alone and in groups, will lead us to Shipapo, but not if we are daunted or impatient, owing to our cultural misconceptions about time. We think we have "so little time." Our time is "taken up" with duties and demands. But there is no *time* on the Wheel. Time has been transmuted into space. On this journey we are not bound by time's divisions. All is flow, realization, awareness.

Since the Great Medicine Wheel comprises all that is, knowledge and understanding of the Cosmic Blueprint is necessary. The more we grasp and can identify with the Plan of the Work, sometimes called the Tracing Board, the better we can travel. There are analogies to help us, suggested exercises, usages, methods of proceeding, but we must discover these for ourselves. It is an individual experience, the journey of the alone to the Alone.

There is one sure way to proceed. Like Dante, like all travelers before us, like Christian in the Pilgrim's Progress, like Everyman, we must start in boldly and persevere with determination. Some will go quickly from stone to stone, from stage to stage. Some walk, some run, some fly, some find water between the stones and swim. Some may only reach the first stone. Others don't manage to leave the circumference. It is always an individual experience.

It has been said it is better to journey hopefully than to arrive. I take this to mean that full awareness of each stage enriches the arrival.

Here are skeleton notes of the process as I experienced it, but all must outline their own guidelines and put them into practice.

Stages

1. Finding one's place on the circumference by whatever method, Sun Bear's, Dante's or another.

2. Going in and coming out. Warm-up exercise.

3. Going in carrying someone or something to be healed. Placing the problem in the Center, leaving it there.

4. Coming out.

5. Going in to get the problem, now dealt with by Those Above; bringing it to the circumference, blessing and releasing it.

6. Going in with all that one has gathered (in knowledge) of the mineral world, leaving it in the Center. Coming out.

7. Going in with all that one has gathered of the plant world, leaving it in the Center. Coming out.

8. Going in with all that one has gathered of the animal world, leaving it in the Center. Coming out.

9. Going in with all that one has gathered of the human world, leaving it in the Center. Coming out.

10. Going in with the superhuman world presences, leaving them in the Center. Coming out.

11. Going in with all of oneself on all the planes of being. Staying in the Center with all that one has placed there for an act of worship and rededication.

12. Leaving in reverse, gathering superhuman, human, animal, plant and mineral. Bringing these to the circumference, blessing and releasing them.

13. Going in for a final act of worship, alone to the Alone. Leaving, bringing oneself back to the circumference.

14. Joining with all on the circumference in a great act of worship, thanksgiving and release.

Later stages come when we are familiar and at ease with these first meditations and exercises round the

Wheel. The Sun Dance, when we come to that great annual renewal sacrifice for our Mother Earth and all our relatives upon her, adds color, sound, motion, the surging powers of drumming, chanting, dance, to the experience.

回回回回

This outline, like the preview of a course presented to a group of students, is not intended to be gulped down at the first session. The interrelated stages must be taken gradually, one at a time, according to the needs and circumstances of the people traveling the Wheel. Working any one of them in depth is enough for a session or several sessions, especially when space is given to individual reports of the journey at the end of it. This is a valuable part of the experience, when insights are shared and growth mushrooms.

In working with groups it is good to ask people selected at random (if there are too many to include everyone) how the experience seemed to them, what they saw or heard or felt, calling on someone from each of the Four Directions. Some will see colors, hear sounds or encounter Beings. Some will experience deepening awareness, or receive the answer to a problem. People will benefit from sharing what they travel through.

One important milestone on the Wheel comes when it rotates, another when it upends before us. These experiences do not normally come at the beginning of the "course." It is helpful to encourage people to practice in their homes on smaller Wheels.

Another encouragement is to invite each participant to choose a stone from the Wheel, after the meditation is over. This stone can become the center stone on their Wheels, or be carried by them as a power stone, a guide. So far in the workshops and seminars I have given in different parts of the country, I have not known two people attracted to the same stone. We have noticed, too, that the number of stones and the number of people seem to work out numerically in divisions of four. Thirty-two stones are the minimum but sometimes we are led to lay out more, on the circumference. The circle of seven, the paths of four and the central Stone remain the same.

I have had as many as fifty participants and as few as eight. These are matters for the Grandfathers and Grandmothers to arrange, with the Deva in charge of the Wheel. A great deal of intricate planning, interweaving and meshing on all the planes goes into getting everybody there who should be there. The element of free will and freedom of choice also has to be reckoned with. Usually I don't know beforehand how many people will be seated at the Wheel. These are matters best left to what we foolishly call "chance" although we ought to know by this time that there is no such thing, only the law of cause and effect, set into motion by our choices.

Stage by stage the spiral journey leads us to the entrance of the Shamanic Otherworlds, *Shipapo*, from the Tewa *Sípapu*, the Hopi *Sipápuni*, leading down to the place of the Beginning. Next to the sunken fire pit in the kiva is the small hole in the floor, called *sípapu*, from two words *navel* and *path from*, referring to the umbilical cord from Mother Earth and the path of man's emergence from the underworld.

Shipapo has a wider meaning, but until we have absorbed the groundwork of our studies of the Medicine Wheel and made the practice of them first-nature of our beings and our daily living, we should think of the next turns of the spiral way only in anticipation, as a freshman might consider postgraduate work. It is there, ahead of us if we choose, but first, as for the freshman, come tests, examinations, trials.

We should be ready for these but it would seem we seldom are. If we knew in advance the reasons for these trials, the right choices we should make, and the outcomes depending on them, they would not be tests, and our growth would not be as great as it might be.

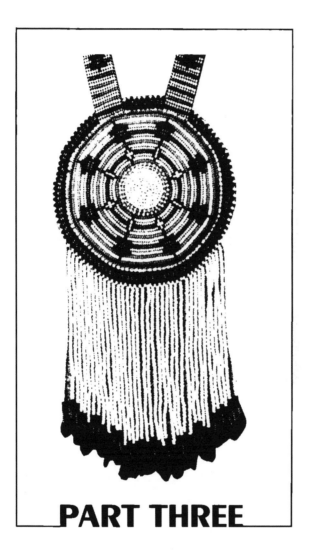

PART THREE

3

One of these hard tests, leading to deep realizations, came to me in 1974, nine years after I received the Pipe and started to "take care of the people." I had offered to be a channel. The offer was accepted, and I was put to use. Suffering people, with little and great miseries, were coming to me, hungry for what they needed, help and guidance on the paths they traveled, or sometimes simply for a listening ear.

I had not planned this sort of role. I was not fitted for it, it was disconcerting, it went against the grain, but it worked, and who was I to resist the Grandfathers? Still I felt uncomfortable. I had a notion, it was more than that, a conviction, that sages, healers, helpers of any kind, should be full of radiant health themselves, and I was not. I had never been. In this life, for this time around I had not earned the blessing of a strong and healthy human overcoat. From birth, through childhood, adolescence, on through life, accidents, illnesses, operations, setbacks, were the accepted norm for me.

I had come to the Native Americans because I was ill, and their Medicine Men had doctored me, time and again, for major and minor ailments. I felt confident that I could recover from anything afflicting me in Eagle Man's Sweat Lodge, but I also knew that he was surrounded by his own people who needed help more than I did and had nowhere else to turn. We decided that beside the doctoring sweats I should also go to a surgeon friend. The two men knew each other. The surgeon had taken a growth off the Medicine Man's eyelid. In return Eagle Man, who is also a sculptor, though he modestly calls it "whittling," presented the doctor with some symbolic carvings in red catlin pipestone, for his office.

This exchange was already a bridge between two practitioners of widely different disciplines, and I was hoping that a shared patient, referred by a Paiute Healer to a White Doctor, might be another step toward better understanding between people and races. There was still prejudice on both sides in the valley. Conditions have improved since then. Ignorance and misunderstanding are steadily lifting, but when I drove on that fine September day full of golds and russets, it was through a passage between two worlds. I belonged to both, but not completely to either.

Excerpts from the Log Book of my diary.
Tuesday, September 10th.

To the hospital for an upper G.I. X-ray. Tests in D.'s office later. More tests to come Thursday. All my pipes these evenings in the garden are asking for one thing, whichever way it goes, may I fulfill the mission I was sent here this time to do. May I be brave and straight and shining. The only thing to do is to live from pipe to pipe and try to end up well. If it's what I think and I think he thinks, I imagine I will be looked after on all the planes. I've been in two minds, sometimes wanting to go, sometimes wanting to stay. So . . . either way . . .

Wednesday, September 11th.

Day of light eating and castor oil in preparation for the tests tomorrow. In between times I read George Orwell's *An Age Like This.* He mentioned lots of people I knew or of my time, and I am interested in his growth as a writer. I don't understand the communist part of it. I went through hardships and saw the depression in France and was down and out and knew "workers" intimately, but it didn't make me a communist, as so many writers and artists were, out of ignorance of Russia and mistaken idealism. I always thought the two "isms" were the same.

Thursday, September 12th.

Morning in D.'s office, with that painful rectum examination, then a session where he showed me Tuesday's results: "flagrant gout," like *flagrant delicte,* cholesterol all wrong, chemical reactions out of whack, etc. Then to the x-ray room for lower G.I. I bled a lot. They had to do it twice. Then back to D. He said "I have bad news for you," but I think I knew it all along. It amounts to cancer of the rectum, the lower bowel, with probable involvement of the liver, and perhaps the pancreas. We will know for sure on Tuesday. But he and I know for sure now. Remain the choices. He spelled them out for me. Operate, and there are three or four possible results. Don't operate, one sure painful bad road, which may also be the same if operated.

I said, "I must think. We have till Tuesday." He asked, "Do you want me to tell Iren?" I said, "No. I'll tell her and Terry."[1] And I added "Anyhow we don't *know* till Tuesday." It seemed odd and unreal. I found myself consoling him, staring past his shoul-

---

1. Iren Marik, Terry Brengle. See End Notes.

der to the little red stone figures that came from my other world. I have known it subconsciously since the last Sweat. I hope the Grandfathers will give me grace and strength and courage to face it all without being a burden and a disgusting nuisance to everyone.

Friday, September 13th.

After spending twenty-four hours without my liver and lights and rectum, after looking at the world from the point of view of one with only a few months to live, a big decision, to be operated or not, it seems I have a reprieve. D. called me to say so, in those words: "How would you like a reprieve?" I said "Very much," even as I was conscious of a strange feeling of deprivation at being returned from one plane to another, and the world lost its strange, wistful remote-near quality, and I returned to the everyday round, with gratitude and resignation, gratitude that all that pain and disintegration is not inevitably ahead of me at this time.

He said that the pathologist did not think the growth was malignant, the first tests did not show malignancy. So I am to go on Tuesday for another painful and disagreeable examination and more tests to make sure.

Saturday, September 14th.

A test? A foretaste? Whatever it was, a strange experience. I shall try to sort it out. Before the reprieve I caught myself thinking when the bill for the new glasses came in, "I needn't have bothered to get them. I won't wear them long enough." Then I went ahead and paid up other bills I was taking care of by installment. It's glorious fall weather. The blue truck is waiting for the camping I was going to do with Edith.[2] I pass it coming and going on my ways, but do not like to think of it too much. I'm listening to music more than usual, classical and folk. I think I would have enjoyed being of this generation, so much freer than mine, so many more opportunities for young poets, young anythings, than mine.

Indecisions, waverings, shiftings, changes of viewpoints and plans had always been traumatic for me. During the next few days there seemed to be many of these, with only one certainty, even if the tests we were waiting for showed no malignancy, I would still be faced with a major operation to remove the growth, from where it was potentially harmful.

Friday, September 20th.

D. telephoned. It is malignant. The operation is set for Friday 27th. D. seems to think that there is a good chance it will be caught in time, but he would have to say so, honest though he wants to be. I called Terry. She will come. I called Edie, ditto. Then P. and I went up the hill for a Pipe, a strong and gentle one. I picked up Terry's sad and anxious vibrations, Edie's and Iren's too, but my own aren't sad. I am naturally shrinking from the pain, etc, but except for wistful, shocked feeling of being suddenly halted, and wanting to go on, I am serene. It is in Their hands. I am asking the Grandfathers to give me grace and dignity and strength to go through with it bravely, and that it may somehow be turned to good. I would like to write a fine Death Song, one great poem. But prob-

---

2. Edith Newcomb. See End Notes.

ably won't be able to. I have wasted so much time and energy when I should have been writing, but there it is.

Saturday, September 21st.

Long calm day, reading and resting. In the evening Eagle Man and his wife arrived for a lovely visit. Eagle Man was tired. He had worked all morning and was leading a funeral in the afternoon for S. K.'s son-in-law. He said that he was proud of the Indian young men who were there, sober and tall and good. The Legion was there also, it was a big mixed funeral, Cry-Dance last night, Christian service this afternoon, with the Legion's ceremony following it. The K.'s are a much respected Indian family. I asked Eagle Man if there could be a special Sweat on Friday morning, which Terry would give. He said yes. He was his gentlest self. He barked at Pommy (the dog) who barked back, delighted. His wife too was lovely. She is one of the wisest, most beautiful people I know. It was a nice evening.

Sunday, September 22nd.

I spent a much better night, probably from the good visit yesterday. Coyotes howled very near the house. As Terry said when we talked on the phone, "Everybody out in full force." I told her of the Sweat arranged for Friday morning. She was glad they could all be doing something constructive for D. as well as for me.

Wednesday, September 25th.

Woke after a bad night and got up to a beautiful dawn. Had a Pipe, peaceful and strong, asking for grace, courage and dignity and humor, to go through

what's ahead. Edie drove me to the hospital. I walked
in, carrying my Pipe, which I hung on the west wall.
This provoked some curiosity. So did my registra-
tion. When we came to "Religion"? I said "Paiute."
They wrote down "Protestant." I said "No, Indian,
Paiute," and added that I wanted the Paiute Medicine Man to have the same visiting privileges, etc. as
any other priest, and that he would be coming,
maybe often, to see me. The usual long afternoon set
in punctuated by pills every hour. I don't take any
pills, not even aspirin, but did, of course, take these.
Then Terry came, looking tired but lovely, and we
had a good time together, saying some surface, some
not so surface things.

Thursday, September 26th.

I had, in spite of sleeping pill or because of it, a
baddish night last night. The bed is hard and the hospital as usual noisy, lots of interruptions all ending,
"Get a good rest now," etc. but all kind and caring.
Later will come worse things. I offered all of it to be
used somehow for good. Dr. Z. arrived to see me. He
will be the anesthetist. He asked if I had any aller-
gies. I was tempted to say, "Yes, to all conventional,
establishment procedures," but it was too late for
that, so I said truthfully: "Not that I know of, but a
fear of having a mask over my face—claustrophobia
—" He said it would not be that way, nothing on my
face, so I thanked him and felt better, more at peace.
Terry and I had a last Pipe. She asked if there were
any reason why my door could not be closed for half
an hour, and we smoked. I was almost knocked out
by my weakness, but it was a good Pipe.

During this period of transition between B.C. Before Cancer was discovered, and A.C. After Cancer was operated, I was learning basic lessons. For years I had thought and taught that we are guests in the House of the Great Spirit. Now I was abruptly shown that I was no longer behaving like a guest or even a tenant. I had become so attached to my place in the House, my "room," that I had slipped into the skin of a jealous and possessive owner, with "rights," and I was feeling sharp pangs at the prospect of relinquishments. Perhaps I was being put out of my fancied place in the House to make a necessary point.

The second basic lesson I was shown was that since the cancer was there and growing within me long before I began to be used as a healing channel, physical weaknesses and what I had thought of as Karmic justice and in my moments of dimmed understanding as punishment, well deserved and to be accepted with humility and patience, "Sad Patience, too near neighbor to despair,"[3] were no barriers to the work of the committed in the Company of Light. On the contrary they could and would bring increases of power.

This was later brought home to me when I met a paraplegic healing others from his wheel chair, and a chiropractor who had severed his left arm in a seeming this-plane accident, which he and his family and friends resented, until he found other, better ways of healing through his maimed and useless hand.

The third basic lesson was my first conscious experience of the Shamanic tunnel to the other worlds. This came to me during the anesthetic. The Log Book says:

---

3. Matthew Arnold, *The Scholar Gypsy.*

Friday, September 27th.

A pressure on my spine and then OUT, V-vroo-mm into black nothingness, followed by strange impressions of great blocked off areas and strips of black, and something like book ends of stone ledgers closing in behind me. Ahead the narrowing black tunnel. I was flowing through it naked with my arms outstretched, like a diver. I knew that I was going forward and through to Somewhere, though I saw no glimmer of any opening.

꿈꿈꿈꿈

Propulsion into the tunnel by enforced, imposed methods, accidents, operations, shocks, sometimes drugs, rarely take us to the right places, or to the Light. Shortcuts imposed on us by ourselves or others are not a wise way to proceed. It is better to take the slow, sure way of the preamble, of meditation and work around the Medicine Wheel, in constant awareness of our goal "the light at the end of the tunnel." This is a familiar cliché, and like many clichés an instinctive, widespread recognition of a fundamental truth. There is the Tunnel and there is the Light.

The Tunnel is well known to Shamans, who travel through it constantly in search of healing for their patients, or to obtain the help of power animals, or on other missions requiring altered states of consciousness (without the use of drugs). They have many ways of entering the Tunnel and many methods of controlling their passage through it. There is also the Tibetan concept of the Light to be sought and held to after arriving at the doorway to the other world, the Clear Light of the Void, spoken of in the

Bardo Thodol as "such a Dazzlement as is produced by an infinitely vibrant landscape in the springtide."

Friday, September 27th cont.

Then I was back in bed. I saw D. beside me and I said to him: "Tell me the truth." So he told me he was able to take out twelve inches of bowel, contain the malignancy, sew up the ends, no need of that hole and litter bag I dreaded. He called the operation a re-section. Later—Terry says there was a long interval, but none to me—I saw her in the room and asked "What happened?" I meant "in the Sweat" but she thought I meant the operation and confirmed what D. had said. So I asked, "How was the Sweat?" She said "Good. Wonderful." I passed out again and have only a confused memory of kind, skillful hands and voices.

▣▣▣▣

It was made clear to me that I was still an old sergeant of the Irregulars in the Company of Light, and though for now disabled, I was still on duty. Even when I was in intensive care people were coming to me for counsel and asking for blessing. I seemed to be the focus of a flowing stream of power and guidance to friends and strangers, while I was still tied up to bottles and tubes. Terry said I looked like an impressive juke box.

Tuesday, October 1st.

This was the night of Iren's concert.[4] As usual she played gloriously. I know because she had a cassette made for me. I have it here and play to people who want to hear it. At the end she told the audience that

---

4. See End Notes.

she was playing "in honor of Eve who cannot be here tonight." Beside the pleasure and comfort the cassette brings me, I know the stream of healing music helped me, as do the pipes and prayers and sweats.

But it went deeper. Later I came on what Satprem says about music.

> It is a sound that makes one *see*. Poetry and music are an unconscious handling of secret vibrations . . . powerful means of opening the consciousness. . . . a special translation of the great unutterable Vibration . . . if once, just once, be it a few minutes in a lifetime, we hear that Music there, that Joy which sings above, we shall know what Beethoven and Bach used to hear: we shall know what God is because we shall have heard God. We shall not even say anything in capital letters; simply we shall know that *this exists* and all the suffering of the world is redeemed.[5]

Tuesday, October 1st cont.

This was also the day that Eagleman gave Terry her Pipe, a great milestone. Apparently, though the old pipe was only a "commercial pipe," which I had given her in early training, it "had good things in it," all the prayers and the ways she used it, and so she could have this new one. She is delighted with it, so am I. It is small, shaped more like the Micmac pipe, with a lovely white pipestem. It has all sorts of markings on the stone. Eagleman's wife says it is a nighttime Pipe, with galaxy, the milky way, stars, but good in the daytime too.

---

5. Satprem, *Sri Aurobindo or the Adventure of Consciousness* (New York: Harper and Row, 1974).

Wednesday, October 2nd.

Terry told me there was a golden bee that flew round the circle of the rocks in the Sweat, and that she also saw seven black eagles flying south. Eagleman said, "Seven mountain men came, took the sacrifice (Terry's old pipe, burned in the fire), and took it south."

🝔🝔🝔🝔

There were eagles round the hospital during my stay there. I heard that this was unusual. I could see them from my room, also trees and flowers. The Eagle is the Grandfather to this continent of Turtle Island, and to all the world.

In a book I published a few weeks before I went into the hospital, I had written:

> The Eagle, honored in all ages as the messenger of heaven is also, and not by accident, the emblem of the United States, a bridge between two opposing civilizations, and one of the few concepts common to both.
>
> In India he was the Vahana which transported Vishnu and other Sun Gods, like the Babylonian Etana, whom he carried up to Heaven. In Egypt the letter A was represented by an eagle, signifying the beginning, the day, the warmth of life. In Vedic tradition he was the messenger bearing the sacred soma, the ambrosia of the gods, from Indra, the Sky-God. In Greek mythology, he slept on the scepter of Zeus and carried his thunderbolt. In Sarmation art he also carries the thunderbolt and is the emblem of battle, like the Amerindian Thunderbird of whom it is said, "The winged creature which crowns the totem pole is the Thunder Bird and represents the Great Creator or the great Creative Forces."
>
> The eagle is the equivalent in the air of the lion on earth and is sometimes shown with a lion's

head. In alchemy an eagle devouring a lion is the symbol of volatilization, his wings equal the spirit, his flight stands for imagination and spiritual victory. In ancient Persia he was Siena, "the ever blessed, glorious and mighty bird whose wings dim the very heavens."

In ancient Syria the eagle with human arms stood for sun-worship. He also conducted souls to immortality and in general was a messenger, a go-between the earth and unseen worlds. The Christians regarded him as a messenger from Heaven, Theodoret compares the eagle to the spirit of prophecy, and St. Jerome said the eagle is the symbol of the Ascension and of prayer. In several mythologies the eagle's flight, because of its height and its swiftness stands for prayer rising to the Creator and grace descending to mortals.

Freemasons will remember the varied symbolism of the eagle in their higher degrees, and in the Bible there is constant mention of him:

"They that wait upon the Lord shall renew their strength; they shall mount up with wings as eagles."

"The bird of the air shall carry the voice and that which hath wings shall tell the matter."

Dante calls the eagle "the bird of God" and in cantos XIX and XX of the "Paradiso" the eagle explains Divine Justice to the poet.

In Christian churches he is found bearing the weight of great bronze lecterns with the open book upon them, signifying that the eagle carries the Logos, the Word of Life to earth. There are also many images of the two-headed eagle, and of the eagle with a victim in his claws. The first is related to the Janus symbol and is usually shown in two colors of mystical importance, red and white. The second denotes the sacrifice of lower forces and instincts to higher spiritual principles.

His feathers were used by priests and medicine men for ceremonial and individual healing. The Egyptian Pharaohs wore a sacred cloak made of eagle feathers and such cloaks were also used by Amerindians. Eagle feathers were and still are sacred emblems and those who earn the right to wear one are justly proud.

We find the image of his outspread wings everywhere, in all the countries of the world, but especially in this continent of Turtle Island, North and South America. He is woven into baskets and blankets and beaded medallions and painted from coast to coast.

The day on which one sees an eagle circling in the sky is a good-luck day, with some exceptional message or blessing from the "Great Mysterious," for now as in earlier civilizations, the Eagle is the Messenger, and not only symbolically. I have attended ceremonies where, when darkness was complete and after the first round of drumming and chanting stopped, we could hear the sweep of great wings, far above, too high to be reached from the ground, or in any way controlled or manipulated by the Medicine Man, lying bound and helpless shrouded in a blanket, or the people, sitting "in a sacred manner," motionless, crowded close together, so that if anyone attempted to move or to rise, all would have been aware of it.

Some have felt the grip of strong talons on their arms or hands, wings beat about their heads, their cheeks were framed in living feathers. There is also a high piping call, impossible to confuse with its physical counterpart, the eagle-bone whistle used in sacred dancing. It is not like that, nor any other sound that I have heard. I do not believe it could be produced and projected to circle above us by the Medicine Man, from his central position face downward on the ground. People who have never heard it suggest that this and other manifestations are caused by mass hypnotism. Perhaps, but I do not think so.

As the chanting and the drumming resume we can no longer hear the high piping call, but we can

still feel rushing air displaced in a steady rhythm.
When this pulsation ceases, something leaves the
circle. Then the Paiutes say, Grandfather Eagle, after he has looked the people over and given them
his blessing, goes back to where he came from.[6]

This quotation shows the widespread, continuous
recognition of our Grandfather Eagle as attribute and
representative of the Great Spirit, Source of All.
Since writing it, and before that, I had many individual, warm personal encounters with Eagles, golden
Eagles, circling above me as I smoked, black Eagles
accompanying the cars and trucks in which I traveled, Eagle-Hawks, especially the Red-tailed Hawk,
my companion for half a century, who revealed himself to me and others after I received the Pipe.

In the hospital Dante's "golden-feathered eagle in
the sky" circled outside my window "with open
wings and hovering for descent, And I was in that
place . . . from whence Young Ganymede . . . was
snatched aloft to the high consistory" of Those
Above, the Enlightened Ones who rule our destiny
and watch over our Mother Earth.

A little wheeling in his aery tour,
Terrible as the lightning, rushed he down,
And snatched me upward even to the fire.
There both, I thought, the eagle and myself
Did burn; and so intense the imagined flames,
That my sleep was broken off.[7]

It is an experience we recognize. "An idea seized
me" . . . "I was seized by terror" etc. It has passed into the language, a near cliché, though there is noth-

6. Evelyn Eaton, *Snowy Earth Comes Gliding* (Spokane: Bear
Tribe Book Publishing, 1981).

7. Dante Alighieri, *The Vision of Dante Alighieri*, or *Hell, Purgatory and Paradise*, trans. Henry F. Cary (A. M. Dent, 1908).

ing banal about the experience itself. Helen M. Luke says: "This vision comes to Dante when the waiting time is over and immediately before he is carried up to the gateway of Purgatory proper. All busyness must now be left behind because the training for contemplative life is about to begin."

To Dante, becoming Ganymede, Cup-Bearer to the Gods (apprentice helper of the Grandfathers) did not mean becoming a graceful young page handing round ambrosia, it meant entering the searing fire, where the dross in us is purged away through accepted, necessary suffering.

> We are not seized upon by the eagle plumed all in gold until we have reached this point on the mountain of transition to eternity by our own long effort to face the darkness, so that our attitude has radically changed and we are ready to step over the next threshold into a new phase of growth.[8]

Even before we arrive at this stage consciously, or can stay there, intermittently, we can experience the seizure in flashes of dreams and visions, as I did in the hospital. It helped to be reminded by an actual eagle outside the window, and by many memories of actual eagles over the Sweat Lodges, and above the places where I smoke. It helped that my Paiute Medicine Man was of the Eagle Clan. He came to the hospital and also held special Sweats for me. There were Indian friends, too, on the hospital staff, who slipped in at odd moments to visit me. My Pipe was on the wall. No one noticed it, or if they did, there was no comment except once, in the night, in the small hours that loom so large before dawn, I opened my

---

8. Helen M. Luke, *Dark Wood to White Rose* (New York: Dover Publications, 1975).

eyes to find a grave, almost grim, almost hostile dark face staring down at me.

"What is that?"

She pointed to the Pipe.

"That is my sacred Pipe." I expected her to say that I should not have displayed it so publicly, a view I half agreed with, but I also knew that I needed all the reminders of the Transcendent, and all the protections, channels, bridges to the Source of All that I could cling to at this hour.

I started weakly to explain, "If I were a Catholic I would hang my rosary there, where I could see it, or have it in my hand where I could feel it. If I were a Protestant I would have a Bible near, but I am going another way, to the same Source . . ."

She interrupted. "Devil's way," she said. "Why don't you go to the Foursquare Gospel Church? That's where you should go."

"I go to the Sweat Lodge instead, but to the same God."

"God! Do you believe in God?"

"Of course I do. It is the same Great Spirit, Source of all, Creator, under any name. And we are all one family." I thought of a phrase she might know, which many Indians use and which I had sometimes seen mentioned in books by native Americans. Later I said it myself, with others, on entering and leaving a Cree Medicine Man's Sweat Lodge.

"All our relatives."

I said it now, looking up at her drowsily. "And that means everything, rocks, plants, animals, people, unseen forces, everything."

She smiled then, a sudden, sweet smile that changed her stern face and lightened her aura. Bending over me she lifted my legs to a more comfortable position. I fell asleep. When I woke she had gone. I did not see her again, but I thought perhaps one mind was open to the Sweat Lodge not being devil's work and sorcerer's den, and Eagle Man an evil wizard.

Tuesday, October 8th.

Today a stranger arrived with an ancient Paiute bowl. It was large and very old. It had been smashed to pieces and she had received the shards from an old man who found them under a landslide at Buttermilk Meadows. He spent five years piecing them together and had not known what to do with the result. It looked very handsome, with only one small part missing, a museum piece, I thought. She said the old man wanted her to have the bowl and in time she would know what to do with it. Yesterday it came to her that I should have it. I was troubled. I did not want this responsibility. I suggested that it should go to Paiutes of a Sweat Lodge and mentioned Eagleman. She said that what she had heard of him when he came to see me, and at other times, he must be a very good man. I said he was and we agreed he should have the bowl. She left it in a corner of the room and I was very conscious of its strong vibrations.

When the time came for me to leave the hospital, Terry drove the bowl in my car to Eagleman, and I came home in an auxiliary ambulance, driven by a man whose avocation it was to serve the community in this way. Edie sat beside the stretcher. An eagle escorted us for awhile, perhaps the one outside the window, perhaps another. No sooner started than music began, not rock and roll, praise be, not quite my music either, but pleasant and cheerful. To its sounds and the head-turning and smiles of the driver, we went on a scenic journey, magic, wonderful, both sides of the valley shining with new freshness. The days of rain had cleaned and cleared and sun was showing up the colors of the minerals, gold and tawny reds and mauves. Banks of clouds streaked below the crests. It is rare to see clouds in the valley. It was a new and different world.

My arrival to loud blares of triumphant music was spectacular. The friends clustered round the gate watched me lifted off the ambulance and rolled into my room where a hospital bed, on loan from the veterans, was waiting.

I am on borrowed time now. I prefer to think of it as allotted time, and hope to accomplish whatever it has been allotted for. I would like to fulfill the mission I am sent here this time to do. I rejoice and give thanks for the privilege of sentience in the Great Spirit's universe. To be alive anywhere is the possibility of being alive everywhere, and to be alive is the nature of the Creator. All these things, which one has heard and automatically rejected, are different when they have become the simple truth, the statement of an experience experienced. In this way it has been a rich and lovely year.

I smoked my first Pipe since September 26th, in the late afternoon in the garden. It was gladdening to establish contact again, although I never completely lost it. During the Pipe the golden tree outside my writing room, which faces me as I smoke, exploded into a rush of wind and shed half its leaves. What were left looked resolutely beautiful.

It is a lovely and reassuring thing to be reinstated even though one shouldn't need this reassurance. I do. And I bow my head over ascending incense.

Burning sage fills the room with the pungency of the mountains and makes all well. I wonder whether the play on words in the names of things is here too—"burning sage," the consumed poet or wise man, sage, and in French it also means good, the *soyez sage*, of the nursery. No wonder it's so potent a herb.

My resolutions are to work at whatever I decipher of the will of the Great Spirit, under the direction of the Grandfathers. To *remember*—that's the hardest one—to be flexible and not to develop or cling to notions of my own. To do the work, think the thoughts and pray the prayers wherever I am, whatever I am doing, to comport myself as a *guest*, and work as a willing channel between the Healers and those they send to me.

Sunday, November 17th.

We were sitting in Edie's garden when a crow came directly towards us obviously warning of some impending happening. He cawed and he cawed. We looked further and saw two golden eagles circling towards us, a little to the west. As soon as the crow saw that we were alerted, he stopped cawing and flew directly north. We watched through glasses until, as eagles do, they disappeared into the sun. Then a long Vee of white birds came over, not geese—we weren't sure what they were, these "portents in the sky." They lightened our hearts.

Later I saw some illustrations of whistling swans and their flight formation, and recognized what we had seen. Later still the whistling swan became one of my power animals, accompanying my Pipe. This was not my first sighting of the whistling swan. Many years ago, when I was being considered as a postulant in an Anglo-Catholic convent, seven whistling swans flew past my window, flying low for me to see and hear them, at a crucial turning point of decision.

The whistling swan is smaller than the trumpeter swan. It does not trumpet but it has several notes, a silvery, whispering whistle and a louder sound like an ethereal oboe. The swan has many symbolical meanings, and there are shared legends scattered through the arts and literatures of all times. Great poets are swans. Dante's Virgil was known as "the Mantuan Swan," and Shakespeare as the "sweet Swan of Avon" for obvious reasons.

> Dedicated to Apollo, as the God of music, probably because of the belief that it would sing sweetly on the point of death, the white swan was sacred to Venus, an image of chaste nudity and immaculate whiteness. But Bachelard finds an even deeper significance: Hermaphroditism, since in its movement and certainly in the long phallic neck it is masculine, yet in its rounded silky body it is feminine. [I take this to be an allusion to the balance of opposites within each individual aspiring to the Shamanic way, the Ying-Yang completion of the whole.]
>
> This ambivalent significance of the swan was also well known to the alchemists, who compared it with philosophical Mercury, the mystic center and the union of opposites. The essential symbols of the mystic journey to the other world (apart from the death ship) are the swan and the harp. This would afford another explanation of the mysterious song of the dying swan . . . whatever pulled the Sun God's chariot by day, it was the swan that hauled his bark over the waters by night. The relevance to this myth of the Lohengrin legend is self-evident.[9]

9. J. E. Circlot, A Dictionary of Symbols (New York: Philosophical Library, 1972).

The Indian also has his mysterious death song, and his Spirit Canoe; but it was several years before I made the connections between these things and the whistling swan accompanying my present Pipe. As always the Grandfathers give us signs and sounds of themselves to remind us of the Great Spirit, Source of All, subtle allusions, forerunners of ways opening up to come, dependent upon the choices that we make, and the depth of our commitment to the Way.

1975

A quiet New Year's Day. It was bitterly cold with a piercing wind. I could not walk nor go up the mountains for the Pipe. I smoked in the writing room alone. As I was beginning, I heard my name called loudly, outside the window, "Eeeeve," very urgently. I didn't recognize the voice, nor could I tell whether man or woman. I looked out of the window, raising the blind, but nobody was there. So I went to the door—nobody there. I was feeling cold and strange. I locked the door and settled down to smoke. Then a little flashing light appeared behind my left shoulder and darted about like the hummingbird in Sweat. I said, "My Grandfathers I don't know who is calling me. Take this smoke and may it go to where the need is." It was a strange otherworldly Pipe and feeling.

Friday, January 3rd.

At twelve I went up the mountain into the most heavenly sunshine for a Pipe. This evening Francis called to tell me Iren was operated this morning for a kidney stone which had made its way into the urethra. She was in great pain yesterday. He took her to the hospital and operated this morning. She didn't want me to know until it was over but it may have been she who called or someone for her, whom I heard on Wednesday, for that was when her pain began.

Tuesday, January 7th.

A number of new things with the Pipe. Just as I was lowering it I heard the Eagle whistle. I didn't open my eyes, but Elizabeth did and saw a large one circling above us. He made two passes, whistling. I heard it twice. This is the first time that has happened. What a sound it is!

Friday, January 10th.

It will be impossible to write this book (*I Send A Voice*) unless I ignore all reactions—my Indian friends, all—and go ahead. Perhaps it will be posthumous or anonymous. There speaks the coward, because there hovers round one shoulder the wraith of betrayal. It is so inculcated that all these sacred ways are not to be divulged. It is further complicated by the racial problem. Yet, behind the other shoulder a presence which warns the time is right, the people sick, starving for fragments of the truth, for any spiritual food, the necessity to share whatever wisdom one may have, and that a true account of inward and outward growth might feed others. It will be a painful time to go through when it does come out.

Monday, January 13th.

Three of us went up the mountain for the Pipe. We saw two golden eagles circling, and seeming to wait for us. One was a small one, perhaps the one an elder described after my fast, the other enormous, the grandfather of all eagles, and when the sun shone through his feathers it was a glory. After we began to smoke we didn't see them again. I asked for help tonight, for the Sri Aurobindo class. It went off well. There were more young things. They are so touching, like field mice with their bright, bright eyes, their trusting faith. I had to talk about the Army of Darkness this time because Aurobindo brought it up. Their expressions changed. They looked sunk, but later when he tells of the probable necessity for darkness to test and offset light, joy came back.

At the end of the session when I gave thanks for the Army of Light, in which we aspired to serve, and the Army of Darkness because "Darkness and Light are both alike to Thee," I lost one of them. She never came back to the class, and she avoided me, even crossing the road when it looked as though we might meet. Later she left the valley. Years later she wrote from across the continent that she had at last come to understand what the statement meant and she "was all right now." So powerful are words! So careful we should be in using them. How to make careless people realize that to name a person or a thing is to evoke the essence named? People who swear and use what we used to call "stable language," the coarse four-letter words, fill not only their auras, but their living-rooms, their bars and offices and everywhere they go with the stinking substances they evoke and tune into. The contrary is true. Some people fill their atmospheres with beauty, with light.

Thursday, January 16th.

Went into Bishop for errands and to D. for check up. He found a sore that is still oozing in the scar and said it must come out. He looked grave about the pulling feeling I described, but mostly about the sore. When I asked, "Has it come back?" he said, "You mustn't think of cancer as an It. That one is over, dealt with. Whatever comes up now is a new one to be dealt with in new ways." He repeated "Cancer is not an It," and made things worse for me by adding, "It's a They." I said I'd rather have an It than a They, some sinister committee sitting inside my human envelope.

We laughed, but I went home startled and upset. A week tomorrow at 7 a.m. back to the hospital. Out patient this time, local anesthetic which will hurt right where it all still hurts anyway. I can't say I am happy, because it may mean more to come, and I had hoped the one big ordeal was enough and ended the cancer bit for longer than three and a half months.

Friday, January 17th.

We went up to Deep Springs today to show the illustrations of *The History of a Tree* to Dian Mawby who may be doing the lettering of the initial letters, and to talk to her. It was a glorious day and I enjoyed the drive and lunch on Gilbert's Pass and the blue, blue sky, "but underneath I always hear Time's winged chariot hurrying near" and am trying not to be afraid. We had a Pipe up there in the peace and silence on top of the valley.

Saturday, January 18th.

I consulted *I Ching* this morning. I asked: "Is cancer spreading in vital parts of my body?" The answer was revealing:

> If he knows how to meet fate with an attitude of acceptance he is sure to find the right guidance. The superior man lets himself be guided; he does not go ahead blindly, but learns from the situation what is demanded of him and then follows this intimation from Fate. The superior man gives to his

character breadth, purity and sustaining power so that he is able both to support and to bear with people and things.

So much for the attitude I should have toward what would be demanded of me, and the listening ear I should turn to the promptings of the Grand-fathers.

I Ching continued:

As the light-giving power represents life, so the dark power, the shadowy, represents death. When the first hoarfrost comes in the autumn, the power of darkness and cold is just at its beginning. After these first warnings, signs of death will gradually multiply, until, in obedience to immutable laws, stark winter is here. In life it is the same. After certain scarcely noticeable signs of decay have appeared (like the sore on the scar)—they go on increasing until final dissolution comes. *But in life precautions can be taken by heeding the first signs of decay and checking them in time.*

That was what D. and I were trying to do. After more graphic descriptions of the present condition my envelope was in:

Work on what has been spoiled. Decay. The Chinese character *Ku*, represents a bowl in whose contents worms are breeding. This means decay.

It also, I thought, meant cancer. The message went on to open a vista of hope based on right action.

What has been spoiled through man's fault can be made good again through man's work. It is not immutable fate that has caused the state of corruption, but rather the abuse of human freedom. Work towards improving conditions promises well, because it accords with the possibilities of the time. But something must be undertaken. Decisiveness and energy must take the place of the inertia and indifference that have led to decay, in order that the ending may be followed by a new beginning.

Then it gave me one of the small assignments *I Ching* and the Grandfathers sometimes toss at those who follow them:

Debasing attitudes and fashions corrupt human society. To do away with this corruption, the superior man must regenerate society . . . First remove stagnation by stirring up public opinion, as the wind stirs everything, then strengthen and tranquilize the character of the people as the mountain gives tranquility and nourishment to all that grows in its vicinity.

(Is that all, Grandfathers, for the superior man to do? *All* I should attend to?) The Superior Man, or of course Woman, is a wonderful name for us. It reminds me of the Tibetan equivalent, the "Oh Noblyborn" the monk whispers in the ear of a dying, perhaps very ordinary human being, who instantly rises to this true concept of himself, as we do to the Superior Man.

There are some books which conduct a dialogue with the reader: the *Tibetan Book of the Dead*, the *Letters of the Scattered Brotherhood* and the *I Ching*. Whenever I consult them, alone, or with a group of students, they speak to the questions, or the situations, or the needs of the hour. Now the *I Ching* continued:

Return. The turning point. The time of darkness is past. After a time of decay comes the turning point. The powerful light that has been banished returns. The old is discarded and the new is introduced. Rest. Allowing energy that is renewing itself to be reinforced by rest. The return of health after illness. Everything must be treated tenderly and with care at the beginning so that the return may lead to a flowering.

The hexagram counsels turning away from the confusion of external things, turning back to one's inner light. There in the depths of the soul one sees the Divine, the One. To know the One means to know oneself in relation to the Cosmic Forces. For this One is the ascending force of life in nature and in man.

I found these answers direct and startling and copied the parts that struck me most forcibly. Then to get ready for the Sweat tomorrow I went up the hill with my Pipe. The eagle was waiting for us on a rock. I put out the offerings for him, corn and sardines, before smoking the Pipe, but he did not fly over during the smoking, not till we were finishing lunch. Then he came sailing above us in a direct and courteous salutation. My heart lifted as it does each time I see Them and I was serene and full of joy again.

It put me in mind of Dante's great Eagle, when it discoursed with him so courteously. I give thanks to the Grandfathers for Their guidance, Their help and Their courtesy and those signs and tokens They give us of Themselves, to remind us of the Great Spirit.

During this interim when, like the first reprieve, tests and x-rays avered that *They*, Cancers, were not in sinister session, I went about the business the Grandfathers entrusted to me. I dealt with those who came to my door, in the ways that I was guided to what I understood their needs to be. Almost daily there were signs and tokens of the Winged Ones' approval and protection.

Wednesday, January 22nd.

The only things worth recording these days of much busyness are the Pipes and where we smoke them. Sometimes up Oak Creek beside the stream, where we often see the Eagles, sometimes my small one, and the water sings loudly when we smoke; sometimes up Onion Valley road to a special place where there is no water but a wide expanse, and where we have been going now for a year; sometimes on back roads coming home from Bishop. The Pipes are always different in their quality, depending on many things, but mostly on my preparation and state of awareness as a channel, and the work to be done.

Sunday, January 26th.

Sixty-two in the shade today, fantastic for January. The blossoms will be in danger of frost. The birds are trying to nest. Sweat at noon. P. took it so it was very hot. It was a Grandfathers' Sweat (the term for thanksgiving) and there was much to be thankful for. I heard a touching thing about H's long Paiute prayer for me last week; she invoked all the spirits, Mountain Men, Hawk, Beaver, etc. and said, "My prayer— Eveleeny die of old age." She is so sweet. She gave me my Indian name. I love her very much.

Monday, January 27th.

Winter is here quite suddenly, as one felt sure it would be. 22° this morning, yesterday 62°, snow on the mountains and all around, and a bitter wind. No good mail and cleaning day! But, even wintry, the view from my writing room window is beautiful. It is only that we have been spoiled the last fortnight with balmy, breezy weather. Four months ago the operation, not forgotten, not outlived, but I am limber and except for reminders, well. A Pipe in my writing room, very strong and reassuring. The great solicitude. Aurobindo evening (I was giving a course on Sat Prem's book on Aurobindo to a group of all ages.)

Wednesday, January 29th.

Nightmares of water flooding into a city. I have always been what the French call *étourdie*. The American translation "dumb" isn't good, because I talk a lot and say some valid things. *Étourdie* is more a case of being deaf, unaware, not with it. Started work on the next radio program. Went to Lone Pine. Saw Elizabeth who told me more about H's prayer for me, and her story, or rather the old legend of the bee that flew all the way up the valley as far as Mono and back, to escape from a red-tailed hawk. When it reached the pinnacles at Mount Whitney Portal, they opened to let it in and the Mountain Men closed them, snap, behind the bee, so it escaped. Edie pointed out that there always seemed to be bees coming when we smoked, and there was also the golden bee Terry once saw in Sweat.

I was not too conscious of Grandmother Bee, but I should have been. The bee is "the divine part of the mind of God" according to Virgil. There are two pages on the universal recognition of the royal and divine bee, giver of honey and wax, and so of sustenance and light, in the *Encyclopedia of Religions* and many other dictionaries of mythology and symbolism. But what I chiefly remember among the Indians is the half amused, half rueful comment in *The Education of Little Tree,* one of my favorite modern classics. Others think so too. I buy it and buy it, but it disappears from the shelf faster than I can replace it, and I am glad of that. It is a book that should be everywhere available to young and old. The quotation I remembered was what his grandfather said to Little Tree:

> "It is the Way," he said softly. "Take only what ye need." . . . And he laughed, "Only Tibi the bee,

stores more than he can use . . . and so he is robbed by the bear, and the 'coon . . . and the Cherokee. It is so with people who store and fat themselves with more than their share. They will have it taken from them. And there will be wars over it, and they will make long talks, trying to hold more than their share. They will say a flag stands for their right to do this . . . and men will die because of the words and the flag . . . but they will not change the rules of The Way."[10]

Sunday, February 2nd.

Not so bitterly cold but snowing all the way to the valley floor. I went for an hour's walk. If I were six people it would be fine. One of them would stay here while one healed, one taught, one lectured, one cavorted and one main one, with me inside it, would go up the mountain alone, and embrace our Mother Earth in blessed solitude.

It was raining as we drove to Sweat, it cleared during the time we were there, coming down heavily again as we drove home. Rain in this desert country is an Event! The Sweat was gentle for me. I am beginning to feel more normal, able to sit up all through it, and not even approaching the end of reserves. I am more and more aware that I must have been ill for a long time before the cancer was discovered—all those times I collapsed in the Sweat, all those queasy feelings. I thought it was just from growing old.

Monday, February 3rd.

Aurobindo day. Before the meeting I had a Pipe in my writing room, and asked that Sri Aurobindo or anyone he cared to send, if he wanted to, might at-

10. Forrest Carter, The Education of Little Tree (New York: Delacorte, 1978).

tend and bless us. I was late getting there, because Terry telephoned to say the date of Eagleman's going to Indiana was changed to April 2nd. The meeting went exceptionally well. At mid point Pommy got up and barked a welcome towards the door from the garden. C. was sitting there. He got up and left the room, as though he was being gently set aside, and Someone or Thing came in and I think took C.'s chair. I decided to go on reading as one would in one's classroom if a Visitant appeared. Many didn't notice anything. Elizabeth did, C. did, naturally, and I. Maybe Diana too. The meeting seemed to be exceptionally helpful to everyone. They all had something to say and said it, as usual, but on a higher level.

Wednesday, February 5th.

This was a glorious day in more ways than weather, which was wonderful, sunny and warm, the mountains covered with snow. I wrote letters and did gritties, then we went up the hill to our usual place. On the road, waiting for us, on a boulder, sat my small eagle. I have never seen him so near. Speckled breast, noble head, black wings and body. He was quite unafraid as we stopped the car to look, and stayed for a long pause, then slowly flew away northwards to a tree and stayed there. We went on up and had a most high Pipe, left corn and fish in the usual offering place, and to make doubly sure, drove to the Whitney Fish Hatchery road and up to the stream and left a second offering there.

Saturday, February 8th.

A lovely day. So lovely that we switched the dinner tonight for D. and his wife, to a picnic lunch up the hill. Edie and I went up with some of the food and to set out a place. We smoked the Pipe by the stream.

Then she went down to help with the food and the transportation and left me there alone. This was a balm to the spirit. I am hardly ever alone, and people, groups of them are not my bag. I think "bag" must come from "Medicine Bag," which everyone can have and carry. Presently the caravan arrived. D. flew in. His wife went to get him at the absurd airport Independence has. Iren had made a glorious dinner for tonight. It all came up to make a picnic beyond compare. I think everyone enjoyed it. D. asked me many questions about the Grandfathers, the Eagles, etc. and finally conceded that if I would call the Great Spirit "the System" and not give it a personality and pronouns, he would be able to go towards agreeing with me—a big step forward! He seems contented with my condition. I am not. There is a warning in the winds around me, and the message from I Ching.

Sunday, February 9th.

It rained heavily in the night. Now the mountains are hidden. It is snowing up there. The rain makes everything clean and fresh. The Paiutes speak of a new start and are always pleased with rain. In big cities rain can be inimical. I remember when I lived in New York how dreary it made the days, but in the desert it is at once a comfort and a miracle. The light effect from my window is strange, pale sunlight on budding trees in the foreground, against dark foothills and gray mist. The Sweat Lodge was a little sad and heavy today, perhaps because we were asking help for a brave Indian baby we all love. He has been in a cast for a hip defect. The pin got loose and now the hip is infected and the baby in pain. The Grandfathers will help and the prayers in the Sweat take away the pain at least.

Monday, February 10th.

It was snowing this morning when I woke, but by noontime it had cleared. The sun is out, the sky deep blue, the mountains filled with new fresh snow and my picture window washed so I can see them undistorted. Aurobindo class. More young ones this time, and it went well, not as excitingly well as last time because the chapter was not so challenging. The unseen guest came in, but not so overwhelmingly.

▣▣▣▣

For the next few weeks there were surface comings and goings, people coming for help, a concert to be arranged in Death Valley, and the writing of the current book. Always glimpses of the Winged Ones, and encounters and relationships with Mother Earth. Underneath these, the stirrings that I felt in the sinister committee-meeting room, but none of the tests confirmed them, so I put doubts aside as an unworthy lack of trust in the Grandfathers.

The main event for me was the return of a friend I had long lost sight of, whom I had met when I was, like him, a resident fellow at MacDowell. In the dedication of one of my books, I wrote what I have always felt about MacDowell:

> For the late Marian MacDowell, in gratitude for her courage and wisdom in founding the MacDowell Colony, where writers, composers, painters and sculptors find what they need to create their best works—freedom, isolation, respect for achievement . . . dynamic peace.[11]

---

11. Evelyn Eaton, *I Saw My Mortal Sight* (New York: Random House, 1959).

Later, in my autobiography I wrote:

When I think of MacDowell I think of walking back from my studio, swinging my basket, past an open door with the sound of a flute spilling out, another with a sound of chiselling and hammering, seeing ahead of me a colonist's back and knowing from his walk that his day has been successful. I think of great pine trees, the shadows beneath them, old stone walls, Monadnock in the distance, meals with exhilarating discussions. I think of winter sessions, being whirled to my studio in a snowmobile, the years of the great snow. I think of crackling fires. I think of a small group in Louise Talma's studio,[12] listening to her play with one hand on a tinny piano, and rap with the other on a table, a ghostlike version, a wraith of her *Time To Remember*, and suddenly before us marched the funeral procession for John F. Kennedy, raising goose pimples of remembrance, while she sang all the parts, even somehow the chorus, the faintest dry whispering, yet how evocative! I think of Debby de Moulpied in her studio among the strange floating shapes of her shell-like moving forms, the coloring, the lights . . . the whole mysterious cosmos turning there, suspended from the ceiling on black fishlines.

I think of listening in the library to modern composers who were also performers, playing the great classics. I think of Iren Marik giving a recital there to the "Friends of MacDowell," on the piano where so many composers played. I think of Mack Schleffer playing MacDowell's piano works in the evenings to anyone who cared to listen, and sometimes to me alone. I think of him later, conducting Iren with the Ridgefield Symphonette in MacDowell's Concerto No. 2. I think of replaying the tape of this performance, in the library, and also

---

12. Internationally known composer. See End Notes.

in the California desert to groups of interested listeners who would not hear it otherwise. I think of Iren playing the same concerto with the Fresno Symphony, in Death Valley, for the Bicentennial —an historic "first," a concert of classical music in the Headquarters of a National Park. I think of the astonished audience, and especially of several Indian faces, exposed, perhaps for the first time, to *good* contributions of the white world, instead of the raucous junk featured in many Indian museums as typical paleface culture, along with a heap of trashy stuff, in contrast to the beautiful authentic Indian exhibits . . . a great opportunity lost to compare the best with the *best*, and teach our children and the older public to appreciate and learn from both.

I think of continuity, MacDowell continuity . . . Joseph Wood,[13] for instance, composing *The Progression*[14] in the studio where later I worked and where I was able to play the tapes of the premiere performance at Oberlin, in the room where the music first came to birth, and to play it again in the library to a group of fellows, and later, to far away people in the California desert.

I think of things I learned from what people said, among them: "A number of points have been underlined for me this month (summer 1957) through Paul Nordoff a reminder of *standards* and of THERE . . . also from Paul Nordoff a reminder of reincarnation and Karma, 'every moment you are working out the past and creating the future.' "

I think of Marian MacDowell, a great woman with a great vision, who lived to see the vision achieved in her lifetime and established to last after her death. Started from a small farmhouse with a big barn and a bigger deficit, MacDowell became 'a national monument of extreme interest' to the United States and to the world.

---

13. See End Notes.
14. A Ballet-oratorio for which I wrote the text. See End Notes.

I think of Paul Nordoff, playing on an old up-
right piano in the rain, in the woods, near Mac-
Dowell's grave, to honor her at her Memorial.

I think of his selfless career, as a composer therapist at the service of autistic and retarded children, and of the great legacy he left, in England, in
the United States, in Germany and other centers
for the healing of those who find it so hard to
break through into a "normal" life, and join us in
the school of Mother Earth.[15]

I spent ten magic seasons, summer and winter, at
the colony, over a long period of years, and because
Paul read what I said about it, eighteen years later, in
the autobiography, he was launching himself across
the continent, further than that, from Europe, flying
from some dark disaster that he didn't define, and
since family and friends were evidently helpless, or
maybe part of the calamity, he was turning to a
stranger, yet not quite a stranger. We had shared a
few weeks at MacDowell. He had read my book. It
seemed a frail bridge to trust, across those eighteen
years of separate paths, but he had signalled for help
and he was coming. So I went to meet him.

I borrowed Edie's camper—she was in the East—
and gathered up Elizabeth to help me with the driving.

Sunday, April 27th.

I spent the morning getting myself and the camper
ready to roll. Then Elizabeth arrived and we moved
off to the Sweat. This was the regular Sunday Sweat,
with a doctoring for me, because of the coming tests
and check-ups. L. had made me a beautiful bag for
my healing stone. We drove, after Sweat to Keogh

15. Evelyn Eaton, The Trees and Fields Went the Other Way
(New York: Harcourt, Brace, Jovanovich, 1974).

Hot Springs, and all the good places being occupied, lay in the ditch and washed our hair and clothes. Then on and on through Hawthorne, to Walker Lake where we camped for the night. A large moon came up late. We had our Pipes. While we smoked we both heard Something—Someone approaching behind us, ponderous, slow, gentle, rather formidable. It didn't seem to be an animal. Elizabeth thinks it might be a giant, one of the Big Ones said to be roaming about here now. The Pipe was good. We made offerings and had a restful night.

Monday, April 28th.

We drove on from Walker Lake and nearing Reno decided to go to Pyramid Lake, at least the lower side of it, and then back to Reno later. Pyramid Lake was all that I had heard, all I imagined. There were pelicans flying over us on the road to the lake. Eventually they landed on the far side and were swimming there. We passed the road to Nixon and thought of L. No wonder she always wants to get back there "with her people." Even without people, what a magic place—not Nixon, for we didn't go there, but the lake. Such color, blue, green and blue, with a dividing line between the polluted part and the sacred part, divided by the color of the water. We had our Pipes facing the rock called "The Mother" and left offerings and drove on. The car which had behaved perfectly broke down when we reached Reno, just two blocks from the Ford place. The Grandfathers protected us. Suppose it had happened on any of the long lonely backroads we had been traveling. The trouble was with the pump to the power steering and nobody could fix it. We telephoned Carson City. They couldn't fix it, but told us how to manage so that we could get home. We had just time to change our dirty clothes and rush to the airport.

After I had smiled tentatively at two handsome old gentlemen and been rebuffed, the unmistakable Paul arrived. We greeted each other as though still at Mac-Dowell. He looked very ill and shaken, so ill, I wondered whether we would get him home before his "or *something*" happened, and what to do if it did. We put him on the bed in the camper, and decided to break the journey at Gardnerville. I got him a quiet corner room in the motel. The nice owner let us camp outside Paul's window so that he could call for help if he needed it.

Tuesday, April 29th.

The day was magically blue and clear, the snow and the mountains beautiful. Paul was entranced. He lay on the bed looking out the window. When he joined us in front he told us that his Grandmother had come to him, sat on the bed and said "I don't understand all this,"—she waved round the camper, "but you're in good hands." When we reached Mono Lake he asked to get out.[16] We stopped and he staggered a few steps, raised his hands to the sky, reached down to touch Mother Earth, and stood for a moment looking out over the lake. "Ah," I thought, "he knows that this is a sacred place." Some of my anxiety left me. "Strange," he said as we set off again, "I haven't thought of my Grandmother for years. She was a wonderful woman. She was Indian." Elizabeth glanced at me. The mission was beginning to show unmistakable signs of Those who are managing it. It was a long drive, but so beautiful

---

16. Mono Lake. See End Notes.

that it rested him. We left him in the kindly hands of good friends, owners of a welcoming, old-fashioned inn.

Wednesday, April 30th.

A cloudy day but still some palish sun at noon. I took Paul up Oak Creek to the stream. There were people fishing but they only came just so far. We had a ring-pass-not around us. I invited him to sit beside me but did not give him the Pipe to smoke. The Eagle came and circled over both of us. I had put out offerings with gratitude and I hope he got them. I know he did in essence, but I'd like it to be in fact, too. Paul had slept well and though naturally tired, seemed better. He told me that all the way in the plane he had wondered what on earth he was doing, what craziness was this! But now he knew it was right. He told me he was being treated, drastically, for cancer, but that wasn't what had shattered him. He told me something of the psychic trauma round his work, the betrayals and failures beating in on him all at once, the dreadful timing. He wanted, he had to have, a new direction in his life. I hope he finds it. His book, if one didn't know it already, shows how valuable to the Grandfathers he and his work have been and are.[17] When he left to come here, he felt that all of it might crumble, and that he was too sick and too disheartened to save it. I think he is beginning to doubt this, and to contemplate another supreme effort to pick up the pieces if we can get him well enough to go back to Europe.

I brought him to Iren who played him the *Appasionata* and asked for his advice on her upcoming re-

---

17. Paul Nordoff and Clive Robbins, *Music Therapy for Handicapped Children* (New York: R. Steiner Publications, 1965).

cital. They have the bridge of music, and there is a piano in the inn for him to work on. Already he is looking rested. A few more treatments with the Pipe and I will take him to the Sweat Lodge.

Someone has said that artists are the Indians of the world. They certainly receive the same brush-off treatment from dominant materialistic societies, but the kinship goes deeper than that. It is in their values. It is in their ch'i. I define artists and Indians as those who struggle to bring the things of the spirit into material forms to help others. Shelley called poets "the unacknowledged legislators of mankind." This is also true of Indians, even literally. Much of our Constitution, for example, comes to us from the Iroquois. Today where are we turning, in greater and greater numbers for guidance and help in understanding who and where we are, in relation to the Great Unknowable, the Above One? It is those men and women, in incarnation now to help us, who have managed to retain or to retrieve the wisdoms of the ancient teachings and are willing to share them with those who come "properly prepared" in their hearts to learn. It has to be the heart, not the over-developed "scientifically trained" intellect.

Men and women of Heart, embarked on the great Journey, recognize each other regardless of race, age, or any other transiency. Such meetings are joyful, memorable Rainbow days. The people of the Scattered Brotherhood are indeed scattered, spread out thin, working seemingly alone. It is a shining reassurance when any of them meet, but it is never for long. We are all on bivouac conditions, at temporary rest camps between missions, or loaned to other outfits for some special work. When the occasion ends we are dismissed to our dispersal as the Scattered Ones.

When I took Paul to Eagleman, there was an instant bridge between them. Eagleman said he thought he could help, and arranged for four great doctoring Sweats to start in two days time. We spent the two days getting ready for them, asking Indian friends and whites, to come and help, then buying the supplies, but chiefly in our minds and hearts, asking that it might be a powerful healing, that Paul might be open in all his being to receive it.

Wednesday May 7th.

The first of Paul's doctoring Sweats, a very strong one. I brought in my Pipe and sat next to him. I was acting as the patient's family, "standing behind him." We were seven, with valiant Bill protecting us as doorman. All went harmoniously well. Paul relinquished many hindering bonds and made a full confession. I found it easy to do the requisite "crying" for him. One full-blooded Elder, sitting next her husband, helped mightily to pray and sing. Love was pouring out of all of us to Paul.

The first indispensable step toward healing, especially the healing of cancer, is to release all resentment, to summon up, review and dismiss all that our wounded egos hold against anyone who has ever hurt us, all the recent stabs, and all those "old unhappy far-off things, and battles long ago," so long ago that our conscious memory may have forgotten them, so long ago that they may stem from a previous life. We must release everything, forgive everything, empty it all out, bless and free everyone, including ourselves, especially ourselves, of every guilt. Then we shall be ready, open to be healed, by the Helpers and the Healers (Those Above).

It isn't easy. As I watched Paul struggling to overcome the bitterness of recent psychic wounds, bitterness so justified by all our "normal" standards, all the lower mind's self-pitying, self-justifying reasons for resentment, for "righteous indignation," I began to feel my own wounds waking. I, too, had much to release and forgive, in myself and others. Righteous indignation against evil is one thing, against evil-doers, including oneself, it is to be released and thrown out, "returned to sender"—that is to the opposite Outfit from ours, the powers of darkness, of negation, doomed to be swallowed up in Light (but a long way from that consummation, yet, judging from the battle-ground within).

One good way to dispose of dross, guilts, fears, resentments, etc. is to get rid of them in the Medicine Wheel. Another is to put them into the crucible of the Pipehead, to be consumed, transmuted into smoke. "What happened to so-and-so, to such and such?" "It all went up in smoke." Gone, *not to be recalled.* That is the main lesson for us.

"Crying" for another or others is part of the Indian way of life. There are times for people to "lament," to give expression to grief, so that it can be overcome and disposed of, dismissed to where it should go, not bottled up to fester and bring disease upon us later. It too must go up in smoke.

In the Paiute's Cry-Dance, given to them by their great prophet and Holy Man, Wovoka, there is a time set aside for the Cry of the bereaved. I describe this moment in an account of the dancing.

> There was a pause. A group came out of the house, two men supporting a woman between them. They moved slowly past the singers and the dancers, past the great fire, while everyone stood still and silent. Presently they reached what I had not noticed before, the coffin on its high bier in the darkness, built so that it faced the firelit circle.

Here they stopped. The woman stepped forward alone. Then the silence about us, the silence of the night itself, was filled with her "Cry," the sad, terrible sound of human grief, a lonely, proud, noble, almost cosmic lamentation. It pierced the darkness, it went traveling toward the mountains, it was everywhere.

After a moment others joined in, the singers chanted softly, accompanying her lament. This was her tribute to her dead husband, this was his family's and his tribe's farewell. When it ceased there was another long silence, through which she was gently led back, between the supporting men, into the house.

The dancing resumed.[18]

As must life. There is a time for everything under the sun, the sage of the Old Testament tells us, including the time to remember. But when the sorrow or the joy have been remembered, deeply entered into, celebrated with sacred dance and song, there comes the time to forget, the time to move on, toward the next situation, the next confrontation, on a new turn of the spiral, to be fully lived through.

We are blessed, who follow the way of the Pipe. We have only to give our complete attention to the time between Pipe and Pipe, nothing that went before, nothing that comes after, only the *now* with what it brings to us, to be dealt with.

The *now* of Paul's second doctoring Sweat, after the first one of release and purgation, brought healing from the Grandfathers.

Thursday, May 8th.

Here we went again for the second of Paul's doctoring Sweats. It was Grandfather Hummingbird,

18. Evelyn Eaton, *I Send A Voice* (Wheaton: The Theosophical Publishing House, Quest Books, 1978).

this time. I think of this Being as a Grandmother. No matter, of course it must be both. It was very hot. There were a number of interesting lessons for all of us. When it was over I drove Paul back for a rest, and went up the mountain for a renewal Pipe. Later I hung up the hummingbird feeder, as a slight thank you to all hummingbirds. Four of them came at once and hovered round me. L. gave Paul a beautiful pouch today to go round his neck and carry the bird Eagleman also gave him.

Friday, May 9th.

We have been given two days "rest" before resuming the doctoring Sweats. I went up the mountain, taking Paul to bless the bird and the pouch and to smoke the Pipe with him. It was a beautiful smoking, though the Pipe turned hot and threw warm ashes into my mouth. I took this as a reminder to speak only right, channeled words. I wish I could learn and master that! I am afflicted with whitey's windmill chatter, especially with such a congenial listener as Paul. He seems a different man from the wreck who crawled off the plane ten days ago. He walks with a returning spring, smiles, and is happy composing on the inn piano.

Saturday, May 10th.

Today there was a Sweat for a baby, a few weeks old. She was passed round the lodge, from lap to lap, in the complete darkness. She cried at first, as babies cry when they are christened or circumcised, but presently she recovered and entered into the spirit of the blessings she was receiving from her friends and "relatives." When she reached my lap I gave her Poetry, the power of rich, persuasive words, the joy of hearing them, of using them. She was crooning when she reached Paul's lap. He gave her Music. What a good start for this exceptional baby! She has been in the Sweat Lodge before, many times during the nine months her mother carried her, but this was the first time on her own, in her new human envelope. How good it would be if every baby had this start-off on the journey, inside the mother first, then outside with friends and parents, continuing in this way of life, keeping on keeping on, together.

Sunday, May 11th.

I felt very weak. These days are a strain on the old overcoat. I hear the sinister committee meeting within, raising its unwanted voices. I cannot tell how it is with me, to anyone, especially to Paul. But if we can get him on his feet and shining, anything I and the others go through will be worth it. This, the third of his doctoring Sweats, was very hot. I barely made it. The others were drained and exhausted, too, but it was a strong healing Sweat. Paul was exhilarated. He looks a new man.

Monday, May 12th.

So here we went again for the last of the doctoring Sweats. It was a very good, harmonious Sweat, not so excruciatingly hot this time. H. was there. She had spent the night in the community house as we used to do before the sunrise Sweats. She told Paul to give up smoking "Give back to the Grandfathers something that you like," she said. Paul gave up cigarettes on the spot, and since I told him about the brandy he had begun to rely on to ease his pain, he hasn't had a drink. The pain has let up without it. If he can keep this up his health will be better from that alone. Since this was the last of the doctoring Sweats for him, and he had passed triumphantly, gratefully,

humbly, through them, the coming-out meal was full
of little joys. He had built many bridges between himself and others, and found Indian friends and family.
It was a happy, if a tired, time.

🔲🔲🔲🔲

I wish I could relate all the happenings at these
four great doctoring Sweats in their unforgotten de-
tails. It is not permitted at this time, but I can tell the
results.

The man who stumbled off the plane, crushed and
desperately ill, dying, we thought, walked out of the
last of the Sweats held for him, head high, eyes shining, body moving freely, so restored in health and renewed in spirit, that he was able to compose nine-
teen more pieces for his sick children, and play them
for his friends on the piano at the Inn. Later, when he
had rested, and after a Thanksgiving farewell Sweat,
his family came for him and he was able to return to
England, gather up the shreds of his work, forgive
false friends who had nearly shattered it and him,
and come to his great triumph in Westminster Abbey, where few Americans have been honored.

All the rich pageantry of a noble service commem-
orating his work in England, fifteen years of it, rolled
over him. Royalty was present, silver trumpets
sounded, the collection taken up was presented to
the St. George's Homes for retarded and autistic
children, which he had helped to establish.

When he wrote describing the experience he said
that one of the high moments of that hour was that he
was openly wearing the beaded medallion I had
given him, made by a woman in Wyoming, in a hut
with an earthen floor, and one window out of which
she could see the sacred mountains of her people.
She beaded the colors of the mountains at sunset into

the background; in the foreground the ancient symbols her husband interpreted to her. Paul liked to think, and so do I, that this gracious elder in her modest home was part of that great gathering, her work displayed among the centuries-old treasures of the Abbey.

Monday, June 16th.

Paul's letter with the Westminster Abbey program came today. What a glorious occasion for him! All the fixings. Royalty—(Princess Alice. She must be 150 by now. I remember curtseying to her at Frogmore when I was nine!)—Trumpets. Bach, Shakespeare, processions, etc. All for his work. He wrote a very lovely letter and a note with it. I took the program up the mountains, read it aloud to the Grandfathers and then smoked a Thanksgiving Pipe for the protection and help he has been given, and for it to continue until he returns. There was also a beautiful note from his wife, thanking for all that he has learned and been given here. She must be a fine one.

Paul returned in September, looking better than his first arrival, but in need of rest and recharging. He said his last tests had given him a complete bill of health! So much for Pipe-power, but one must be careful always not to use it for power, or feel gratification, personal, of any kind, only awe and gratitude for the privilege of being used as a channel.

Tuesday, September 16th.

No early Pipe. I slept very badly and woke late. I am in pain these days. I had breakfast in bed. A most beautiful day, clouds drifting over the mountains. Later Edie and I went camping up Oak Creek in the furthest place by the water. It was the most beautiful night. Evening Pipe, moonlight on the mountains, the sound of the rushing stream all night. I love the place, the peace, the big camper, and I could spend every night on the mountain. I had my drum with me and I drummed beside the stream, chanted—(somewhat shakily)—before the Pipe. I did feel a surge of response. The Pipe is a Medicine Wheel, the Drum is another, this time the Wheel of Sound.

Thursday, September 18th.

To town, taking Paul and Iren, to see Dr. D., after an early morning Pipe. My appointment was first. D. listened and asked questions and then issued an order for a whole battery of tests—all those I had in May, plus more. I was a little dismayed, but what else could he do? It is almost a year since the operation, and—I think that sinister Committee sits. Iren had the skin cancer on her nose treated. Paul was pronounced well, needing only rest and food, etc. I shall not know until the 30th what D. decides from the tests.

Sunday, September 21st.

Yesterday when I was looking round the living-room, which is really Iren's music studio, I thought how civilized it was—those two (Iren and Cean) were at the piano, the black dog asleep in front of it, the yellow ceiling and the plain rough curtains, etc. and Schumann, Schubert and Brahms, lieder, healing channels of another era. Classical music, played purely, as the composers, themselves channels, direct it to be played, not "rendered" by ego-swollen "artists," can spread healing forces through entire audiences. Iren is this kind of musician, and the young woman singing for her is another. It was a lovely and touching recital, C. singing, Iren gravely and gently playing the accompaniment. I wafted it to someone needing it, and breathed it in myself, as did Paul. Part of his healing.

Tuesday, September 23rd.

Early Pipe and work on the book, then I collected Paul and took him up over Westgard Pass to Deep Springs College.[19] We went into the library to see Eagleman's memorial figure to a student killed in Vietnam. This is a small figure made out of the pipestone, about seven inches high, a warrior, carrying a "peace" Pipe. When he was asked what his commission would be, Eagleman said "My sons came through safe. I give for free." Paul was deeply moved. The figure stands on a wall bracket above the heads of the readers using the library, a bridge between races. Then we drove on to Gilbert's Pass for its magnificent view, and the early sunset lights, before going back to a good place for a Pipe. By then it was getting dark, and as we smoked the stars came out. Paul lay down on his back to see them. A great bird circled over us. I did not look up to see it, but Paul said its wing sweep must have been at least three feet. He thought it was an owl. He questioned me about the Owl. Was there any reason for so much superstitious fear around it? I said that the Owl did for the world at night what the Eagle did during the day. They respected each other, but did not work well together, since one ruled the night and one the day. They were both communicators of messages between the planes. The Eagle brought messages from Those Above, the Owl from the departed, and perhaps the Lords of Karma.

---

19. See End Notes.

Friday, September 26th.

Back to the hospital for more painful tests. We traveled the back roads and had a dip in Keogh Hot Springs. Here we came upon a poor dog without collar or license, with porcupine quills in its side and paws and mouth. We tried to help him, but finally decided he would be better off with the authorities. Edie asked the Keogh office to call them and they did. She checked later. The dog-catcher had picked him up. It probably means the end for him, at the pound, but to stay where he was and in such pain would be misery too. We put him in the evening Pipe for a merciful transition to the Happy Hunting Ground.

Saturday, September 27th.

Took Paul up the portal road to the waterfall, which was hardly more than a trickle—disappointing —usually it is such a glorious torrent. But the drive up was beautiful and afterwards we had a Pipe, an especially good one, by the big rock on Hog Back. The lights on the Inyo side as we drove home were red and gold and Paul loved this last panorama. He has had a good, rich time here. He plans to come back.

Sunday, September 28th.

Morning worked on the book. Afternoon went to the Winnedumah to hear, with Hattie, Fred and Vernon Miller, the compositions Paul had written there, and also some of his older ones. Very moving. We got the whole vibration of his involvement with the retarded and autistic children and what he can do and does for them. Besides, the pieces themselves appeal to any sensitive hearer. After that we went to the last Sweat for him, which was very hot. He said many warm goodbyes.

Monday, September 29th.

Drove down to Kern to put Paul on his plane. Mission accomplished. He goes away restored to strength in spirit, mind and body, and with a wish to return. Even a few months of recession, or remission, or whatever these lulls of well-being may be called, will give him time to put his work in order and to collect himself for regrouping, and developing new blueprints, etc. I wonder who will come homing in next?

◻◻◻◻

Paul went to Germany to buttress up his work there and in other countries. Then a year and seven months later, he did die of the cancer he and we had held at bay until his work was done and stabilized to continue without him, on this plane. His coming, his experiences here, were indications of the mysterious intermingling ways Those Above weave Their great tapestry out of the substance of the lives offered to Them.

Paul did not forget his Indian friends (nor his white ones), who had taken him to their hearts. After leaving us the first time he wrote:

May 16th, 1975

Dear Eve, You told me that I would find all that I needed here—and how absolutely right you were. Not only what I was conscious of needing—rest, quiet, space, healing, but *true* healing and love and companionship and new bonds of friendship,

great beautiful gifts I could not dream were await-
ing me. Iren—her being, her music, her cooking,
her garden, all so true, made with love. Edie, loyal,
selfless, a light-bearer.

You have been so tremendously good to me. You
send me back—no! I take myself back but with a
new strength, a new connection with "that other
world."

Eve, you are a great woman. God bless you.
Much love and joyful thanks and praise.

His last letter came dated:

December 10th, 1976

Eve, darling friend, the cancer has metastasized in
lungs and bones and I am daily weaker. The pain
is mostly under control . . . I have no energy to
write. This brings my thanks and love to dear
April and Will, Hattie and Fred, and a strong
grateful love to all my Indian friends. We know we
will meet again. A kiss to Edie and Iren. And a
long look of exchanging love between us. I will be
so glad to go, the waiting is long, long.   Paul.

Since then Paul's presence has been felt and sometimes seen in the Sweat Lodge. He is one of those, not
earthbound, but coming near us to help with what is
happening on our Mother Earth. One of our last talks
was about the coming new Hierarchy moving up to
take the places of the old. Nothing is static in the Universe. All are "graduating" into higher states, moving upward, outward. Even the Great Mysterious
Source of All expands, grows, and in some way we
cannot understand, needs our contribution of light
and growth and wisdom to add to the whole.

We spoke of the necessity for integrity and loyalty
if we are to cooperate with Those Above. Paul had integrity and he had loyalty and the love of those who

knew him, however slightly, also he had doctoring sweats from a Paiute Medicine Man. Not many can say that, this time around.

◱◱◱◱

January 1st, 1976.

Woke early and had the first Pipe of the year. My resolutions—on this plane (not entirely) work hard, with joy and discipline on the book, and try to get it finished and in. Then, of course, work as a faithful Pipe-woman. Take care of those who come to me. I realize that I am laying a small foundation towards becoming what I want to become, a teacher in the Scattered Brotherhood. It may take many lives, but I have been led to follow the precepts and build them into myself as I try to teach them to others. I am not feeling well these days.

Thursday, January 8th.

Got up and felt better outdoors with my Pipe. Most heavenly weather, clear, clear blue sky and warm in the sun. I sent the introduction and Chapter I to be xeroxed, and then I went back to bed. I have, ever since September or so, the same "indigestion" I had before the operation, but I'm ignoring it. I feel healthy underneath, not that queer queasy feeling when the committee is in session—still, I would be happier if the "indigestion" cleared up. I'll try not eating while the girls are away, or at least not so much! But the pipes, thoughts and reading all serene and good. It's just a small karmic *mauvais moment à passer*, I expect. Dion Fortune's *Sane Occultism* underlines "two qualities—serenity and courage." She also says: "the character of the adept—he is a soldier-scholar, dedicated to the service of God."

Sunday, January 11th.

Woke feeling pretty poisonous and poisoned. Made the mistake of reading a health book and developing extra symptoms. Edie to Sweat, where she received her Pipe, came home and told me about it. She wept on Evelina's shoulder. She gave me lobelia this evening. It knocked me out, and later got to my liver and lights and rushed all over them like the little men of the mountains! I went out like a patient of Dr. Z. only without that VROOOMMM into the dark. Woke at 3:00 A.M. and took another cup and this time the effect was less (I had two cups with the first dose). Slept well the last part of the night.

Monday, January 12th.

Donna gave us the lobelia. It's the same as the Indian tobacco which grew in my corner and of course got rooted up by those fanatic gardeners, M. and M. Naturally it's good to smoke and I loved having it there with its little white flowers. But I think we have some seeds and it may spring up as it did before.

⊡⊡⊡⊡

During this time I was busier than ever. Many more people, young and old were coming to me for consultations and some for training in preparation to receive their Pipes. I was also speaking here and there, trying to write *I Send A Voice*, giving a regular Monday course, and attending Sweat Lodges.

Monday, January 12th. cont.

I had my Pipe in the garden, well wrapped up, Pommy beside me being very good. After lunch I went heavily to sleep and didn't wake till twenty to six, just time to get into my red dressing gown with the rich flowers down the front to give me strength, and get over to the group. It was a good meeting. My voice held out. I read Dion Fortune and commented. The discussion was very good. Everyone was there plus a new one. I held the meditation and then left. Edie asked the child to open the book, *The Letters of the Scattered Brotherhood.* It opened at the Primer chapter, right for her and for the others, too. They are all being assailed by temptations and pulls away from here, poor lambs.

Tuesday, January 13th.

A glorious day. I had Pipe in the garden to thank for the blessings last night. I must tell the group next time that "commitment" doesn't mean anything grim, nor that someone commits us. It means *intent,* a real and more or less steady wanting. We went up the mountain with lunch. It was heaven to get up there again, and just as we were arriving at the upper smoking place, there he was, a big black eagle waiting for us on the tree. He drifted off after a pause, to a tree a little further away. I put out corn and fish for him, and then we smoked. This time, since I had smoked my Pipe this morning, I used the little Micmac Pipe. Edie had her new one. The little Pipe was a short smoke but it was a happy Pipe and a happy time. Later I saw the eagle again with his mate on the rocks. He circled and circled and went up toward the offerings. Later still we saw them both on the rocks as we drove down. So reassuring. The Grandfathers are kind and courteous with these signs and tokens of themselves, to remind us of the Great Spirit. I need all the reminders I can get.

The time came when the facts that I was busy thrusting away from me and the symptoms I ignored as "indigestion" or "something in the food or water," showed up in a series of tests, confirming another session of the sinister committee.

D. talks of liver scans and chemotherapy. I say no, there must be other ways and I will find them. He insists and so do I. We part soberly for me to think it over. But I have thought for a long time, and seen too many friends go the chemotherapy way. It kills more than the cancer cells, and can inflict atrocious pain. I do not believe in it, nor in the general attitude and approach of the Established ways of attempting to heal. As Donald Sandner says:

> Scientific healing often ignores the patient's humanity: I have heard an illness referred to as a "beautiful case of bleeding ulcer"—sometimes in front of the patient. The patient is evaluated as a biochemical machine, and the sick and dying are placed in barren whitewalled rooms surrounded by machines and penetrated by tubes that have no relevance to the patient's tremendous emotional experience.[20]

He also says somewhere else in the book that for tuberculosis or appendicitis or cancer in its early stages, he would be quick to avail himself of what he calls "modern medicine." But for "one of those maladies for which science has no specific cure, like cancer in its later stages or some psychiatric illness" [he would] "prefer the symbolic healing of the Navaho."

I do not believe that Navaho healing is "symbolic." I believe it is actual, like the doctoring Sweats and

---

20. Donald Sandner, *Navajo Symbols of Healing* (New York: Harcourt, Brace, Jovanovich, 1979).

ceremonies of other Medicine Men and Women of many tribes. I believe these "symbolic" healings are nearer to the truth of healing than the "scientific" methods approved by the AMA. I realize that Sandner used the word "symbolic" to underline the use of symbols in native American healing, but all healing, even the orthodox western medicine, relies on symbolism to some extent. The point missed by "scientific" practitioners of "modern" medicine is that we are more than our physical envelopes, that symptoms appearing in our overcoats are at the end of the road of disease, the results not the causes, the working out of the law of cause and effect, Karma, on our lowest levels. To treat the symptoms is to deal with the least important part of the problem. They will disappear when the real malady in the Spirit, that which has thrown us out of harmony with the Source of All, is healed, and when that healing filters through our mental, astral, etheric envelopes to the physical body.

White Eagle[21] has said:

> It is not enough that we bring you the power which will lift you up and give peace of mind, strength of body. You on your part must strive to realize your true life. You believe in an invisible life, an invisible power which will heal you of aches and pains, inharmonies, confusion; but this power needs to have a point of entry. You have to prepare your body, your mind, your soul for the inflow of this divine healing. There are many who seek healing without recognizing this fundamental truth that they are spirit; that they have as much to do with their own healing as any healer who tries to help them. It is not in accord with divine law for the body to be healed completely

21. White Eagle. See End Notes.

without the soul's cooperation. Before the body can be wholly restored you must play your part; the soul must learn the lesson sickness was designed to teach. Pray therefore that you may understand the cause and purpose of your sickness or unhappiness; and remember that whatever your karma it is good, it is an opportunity given you by divine law to grow in spirit.

Bodily sickness is the result of inharmony in the soul; thus to restore bodily health we must work through the soul, or there will only be a patching-up, a temporary relief.

And he continues later:

Remember what we have told you of the cause of disease and the source of all healing; remember also that your habitual thoughts either create or destroy. Lack of harmony in your thoughts or in your life brings disease; harmony brings health. Therefore let go all resentment, fear and criticism. Hold only the positive thought of all-good, God, and light will flow into you.[22]

D. cannot help me, since he thinks of people as bodies, who may or may not have souls, and that the question is irrelevant and we should get on with chemotherapy, the sooner the better. He is a good friend, a skillful surgeon, sincerely attached to his patients, emotionally involved with some of them (I have seen him weep when a young man died). He did his best for me I am sure, and would continue generously with time and care, but I cannot go his way.

Eagleman says, "If you want to stay, you can stay. The Grandfathers will help you. If you want to go, you can go. They will help you over. But you've got

22. White Eagle, *Heal Thyself* (Great Britain: The White Eagle Publishing Trust, 1962).

to make up your mind. It's up to you." I answer, "I will do what the Grandfathers want." He says it isn't that way, it's for me to want and tell them what I want and work for it. He says it angrily. I cannot make him or D. understand how it is with me. Each, I think, feels I should go only *one* way (that familiar trap "I have the only truth"), though they respect each other, and Eagleman sent me to D. Both men are hurt. They feel I am failing them, a strange reversal, surely.

And how do I feel? Bewildered, less prepared to go than I was last year; the book to finish, the groups to teach, beginning to move forward; people coming increasingly for help; the family, the friends, the being needed—what anyone standing in these mocassins would feel, I suppose. The overcoat letting me down, the bone, bone-tired waking each day to nausea, weakness and pain. I'm set apart, a little away from everything, no one understanding, or if they understand, unable to reach me. They feel impatient with me, or with the situation. It should be temporary. I should "get well, *or something*," as I heard a woman wish for her husband. I do understand that point of view. If this is my "or something" the timing bothers me. I'm just beginning to master abc's, I'm being put to use, usefulness seems to be going on, no matter what, and I don't look the way I feel. I look well. The Grandfathers throw an illusion round my envelope. I'm not as much afraid as others seem to be. Yes, of not finishing up well, of leaving so much undone, of pain, and a little of the actual process, but of death, no. I feel with Emily Bronte:

> No coward soul is mine,
> No trembler in the world's storm-troubled sphere:
> I see Heaven's glories shine,
> And faith shines equal, arming me from fear.

O God within my breast,
Almighty, ever-present Deity!
Life—that in me has rest,
As I—undying Life—have power in Thee!

Vain are the thousand creeds
That move men's hearts: unutterably vain;
Worthless as withered weeds,
Or idlest froth amid the boundless main,

To waken doubt in one
Holding so fast by thine infinity;
So surely anchored on
The steadfast rock of immortality.

With wide-embracing love
Thy Spirit animates eternal years,
Pervades and broods above,
Changes, sustains, dissolves, creates and rears.

Though earth and man were gone,
And suns and universes ceased to be,
And Thou wert left alone,
Every existence would exist in Thee.

There is not room for Death
Nor atom that his might could render void:
Thou—Thou art Being and Breath,
And what Thou art may never be destroyed.[23]

I have used for myself and given to others to use, the second and last verses, as mantras, separately and together. They work.

What a benefit it is to have an old-fashioned learn-by-rote education! Under the surface doings of life there are the singing lines of the Swans, the poets, the apt wisdom, the compassionate "I too," and the music. So that we, inoculated with the great lines of the great, when we were young, go companioned always by the Birds of God, who were once men and

---

23. Emily Bronte, "Last Lines."

women like us, singing their ecstasies and agonies, our ecstasies and agonies, for us, who can only chirp.

"Out of my great sorrows I make my little songs." I don't remember which cygnet said that, Heine, I think, with humor and humility. I chirped something like it, when I wrote *Time to Listen*.

> Out of our urgencies we leave
> small words behind
> in corners of dim libraries
> for those to find
> who circle like ourselves
> the edge of things
> and disregarded have the time to read
> and time to listen if a songbird sings.[24]

Even to chirp is to join the great chorus. But now I must decide what to do, since I am turning my back on orthodox and expected-of-me ways, to take my envelope's fate into my hands, and go upon what amounts to be a vision quest, not so much for health, as for coming to a graceful conclusion. I know of others with terminal cancer, who have managed outside orthodox medicine, to live longer than they were expected to, to wind up their lives and their affairs, like Paul, and to make the transition at peace and satisfied. I must try to do the same. I decided to go to Tecopa, for a start, since first comes purification.

⊟⊟⊟⊟

To reach Tecopa from where I lived it was necessary to cross Death Valley, entering it over the incredible winding descent of Panamint Springs. This is an awe-inspiring, spiritual experience at any time,

---

24. Evelyn Eaton, *Love Is Recognition* (Georgetown: Dragons Teeth Press, 1978).

particularly at the start of a vision-quest. In fact it is a vision quest whenever one drives over it. As for those hardy ones who make it on foot, it can change their lives profoundly. I know a man who went through a four night fast (which means also three days of torturing heat) in Death Valley, in June when the temperature was in the 120s. He called me only when he emerged to spare me the anxiety of knowing that he was doing it, and both of us the strain of disagreement.

I would have warned him against a need he may have been feeling, to overprove himself a man. He was training to be a midwife, for sound reasons, but people still in the Piscean Age are confused and confuse others about "suitable professions" for men and women. Some of these vibrations of limitation may have rubbed off on him and made him feel he needed extra reassurance. If I had known what he was planning, I would have had to point out that no one was encouraged even to drive at night in air-conditioned cars across Death Valley in the height of summer; that to walk in and spend four nights and three days holed up somewhere among burning rocks or burning sands, without water, food, or sleep, was to risk his valuable, needed life, and perhaps the lives of others sent to rescue him. I would have said all this to no avail, and spent four nights in prayer and Pipes, sustaining him, as I have sustained other fasting people. He was a grandson, one of several men and women adopting me as grandmother. I have four grandchildren and two great grandchildren of my own, and at first I was startled and a little shy to find myself enveloped in bear hugs by bearded strangers, or kissed enthusiastically by smiling girls, hailing me as "Granma!" Soon I grew to love both hugs and huggers and to be proud of the extended family. This is as near as many of us get to the relationships of tribal life. This is what the questing young mean when they say they "need elders." Of course they don't always listen when they find us. An elder has to be really old, unshockable, willing to be a listening ear and never "an authority figure." Authority figures are what the young—and others—are running from. Even if we manage to be acceptable elders, our young ones come and go like starlings, round us.

I am always glad to have one or two arrive to share the Pipe or the Medicine Wheel or whatever is happening. I am also glad sometimes to be alone, or with another elder of similar memories. We are all of us contemporaries, with different sets of memories, whatever our years of being here may be.

I remember Tecopa as it used to be decades ago, before it became a winter haven for people of a certain turn of mind; when the healing waters gushed out of the ground and there was nothing but a flimsy bamboo screen around them. Now there are bath houses for men and women, with exterior walls and cement divisions between the baths, and camp-grounds, instead of the haphazard ways and places we used to park in. There are regulations pasted up on boards, a community house, a health center and some "authority figures," but the basic realities, the magic essence of the place and the healing properties of the water remain. They will, so long as we respect the conditions of the legacy old Chief Tecopa bequeathed to us. He was the last tribal keeper of the sacred waters. He left them to those who would "come here for help and healing with right hearts." He said that so long as the waters were respected and no money was asked for them—"the Grandfathers don't hear money"—the blessings would continue.

But there was to be nothing commercial around these waters.

The baths are free, and the healing powers still flow through them as many people could testify. Long may Chief Tecopa's injunctions be respected and the custodian presences of those who still take an interest in preserving them be satisfied. If they are desecrated by the sort of treatment many sacred hot springs are given nowadays, where junk and filth of every sort pile up around them, and we are almost glad to see old beer cans as being least repulsive— then the spirits of those places, the devas, the custodians, the guardian powers, call them what you will, disgusted and affronted, move away. The waters they have cared for sicken and change. So far Tecopa is still the home of healing nature spirits.

We arrived there at night, under a growing moon, and had the baths to ourselves. I was able to spend my first hours of preparation for healing, in and out of the waters, and lying on the platform under the wide sky, giving thanks and praying to be able to release all dross. Toward the small hours we went back to the camper and I slept well and dreamlessly.

PART FOUR

4

*The Shaman is a healed healer who has
retrieved the broken pieces of his or her
body and psyche and, through a personal
rite of transformation, has integrated many
planes of life experience.*

Joan Halifax in Shamanic Voices

*I am not a Shaman, as I have neither had
dreams nor been ill.*

Ilkinilek, Ibid.

Water running in cool streams, water surging in hot
streams, water spraying up in fountains, water in
rivers, lakes and seas.

Limitless and immortal the waters are the beginning and end of all things on earth.[1]

Zimmer

Without divine water, nothing exists.

Zosimus

In all the myths and accounts of the creation that
have come down to us, water is the first substance
out of which the earth emerges. From the first chap-

---

1. Heinrich Zimmer, *Myths and Symbols in Indian Art and Civilization*, Bollingen Series, Vol. 6 (Princeton: Princeton University Press, 1971).

ter of Genesis when "the spirit of God moved upon the face of the waters," down to the Paiute account:

> At first the world was all water. Then the water began to go down and at last Kurangwa (Mount Grant) emerged from the water, near the southwest end of Walker Lake. As the water subsided other mountains appeared, until at last the earth was as it is now.

Water is the primal condition. Out of the deeps we come and all things come. The first initiation is the water initiation.

> There is evidence that the final act at Eleusis was the setting up of two vessels which were tipped over, so that the water flowed towards the east and the west, the directions of birth and death. Thus the ritual began and ended with water, symbol of the unconscious beginnings of all life and of the wise spirit of the conscious end—the living water "springing up into eternal life."

White Eagle says: "It is not only the cleansing water but the human soul itself which is signified by the water element."

Great and small Swan poets knew these truths and sang of them down the ages. Two of the best known in the Western English-speaking world came to my mind as I swirled in the Tecopa pool:

> Though inland far we be,
> Our souls have sight of that immortal sea
> Which brought us hither.
>
> Wordsworth

> The moving waters at their priestlike task
> Of pure ablution round earth's human shores.
>
> Keats

Pure ablution was what I was trying for, sometimes alone, sometimes among bevies of silent, or some chattering, nudes; always with inner appreciation of the guardian presences, Tecopa himself, and others, always with contrition for the pollution and misuse of water across this land and across the world, always with gratitude for the healing taking place in me and in the people round me.

At the pool I noticed a majestic woman, teaching Tai Ch'i to the bathers, giving Joh Rei healings to some, and radiating sunny warmth and strength to everyone. Presently I met her, at the small health center, and she invited me to come to her studio and see her pottery. There she also gave me Joh Rei treatments. We became friends. Her pottery was especially noble, and her blue-green glaze exceptionally fine. She told me I should go to the Kelly Institute, in upper Washington State, to learn of another way of dealing with cancer, through a fundamental change in eating habits.

I was ready for fundamental changes. The idea of a vision quest journey towards a definite touch-down place in the north appealed to me. The Grandfathers had sent me the perfect traveling companion, and right hand, in Edie Newcomb. We wrote asking for information and for an appointment.

Before the answer came there were wind-up things to do. Places where I had promised to speak, places I was asked to bless, lodge meetings where I must preside,[2] and other everyday obligations.

April 11th, 1976.

A beautiful day. We got to the Base,[3] signed in and went to take our place in the guided procession to the petroglyph canyon. It was an interesting drive. The

2. International Co-Masonry. The American Federation of Human Rights.

3. The Naval Weapons Center at China Lake.

country is different, from ours. The Joshua trees bigger and better than anywhere I have seen, probably because few people can get in to bother them. There were beautiful vistas and the canyon was exciting. The people spoiled it for me a little, I know what the trees must feel. People prevent our getting into reality. But with Edie on guard I managed to do what Eagleman had asked me to. I hid behind some rocks to smoke the Pipe, with some distractions and apologies to Them. We scattered tobacco everywhere we walked, surreptitiously, through holes in our pockets. I did take some photographs, of some of the most striking petroglyphs, since my coverup made me a photographer. We felt the mission was accomplished.

Monday, April 12th.

We smoked our pipes on the top of the mound near where we slept, among the Joshua trees, with a wide view. There was a dead cow in one of the most beautiful groves. I thought of the Indian prayer, "when it is appointed for me to suffer, may I take example from the dear well-bred beasts and go away in solitude to bear my suffering by myself, not troubling others with my complaints." The cow still looked beautiful, its skin a glossy brown. Then we drove slowly home, stopping in a place to the right of Little Lake, among lava flows, to bless it, to eat lunch and sleep. The wind got up. It grew dull and dark, snowing on the mountains and heavy with promised rain.

Tuesday, April 13th.

It's raining today as I begin preparing for the Kelly cure as instructed. I had a Pipe first, in the garden, by the fence, where nobody can see, but where I can unfortunately hear all the noise pollution of this little desert town, nothing like the noise pollution of bigger places, but still distracting. This Kelly purging is distracting too, and strenuous, but I know will cleanse and help to heal me. I must make full use of it.

Friday, April 16th.

This is the first day of my fast, yesterday the last day of the purging. Semi-fast compared to the Indian ones I have passed through, and of course my human envelope is weak and has discomfort. But the Scattered Brotherhood encourages me to hope for lighter vibrations and more freedom. The wind sweeping through the valley has blown away the smog. The sky is clear and though it is still windy, it is beautiful. I am sorry for the trees and the flowers. I hope the fruit will not be lost as it was last year.

Monday, April 19th.

I ate today for the first time, a normal breakfast, and then the usual carrot juice etc. and salad in the evening after I had given my group session. It went well. J. came and brought a new woman with her. Both contributed some interesting comments, but both are liberal-leftists, unable, usually, to believe in a Great Spirit Creator. I was feeling very weak after the long fast, but I improved and got through it pretty well. It is here, to hand, to be done, so I try to do it, and hope something will spread out and prove worthwhile to them.

Tuesday, April 20th.

A sultry spring day. Second day of eating anything. Morning I wrote letters, hedging ones, not to take on new obligations, some postponing old ones. One to Aspasia saying that I would come to the Hambidge Center, as I had promised . . . if . . . if . . . there is always that IF. Then up the mountain to a new place by another stream, not so fierce and forceful as the one we usually go to. I can imagine what this region must mean to city people. We are so lucky to be able to go up every day if we want to.

Tuesday, April 27th.

The flowers are tremendous in the garden and in my writing room. Full summer suddenly. Lilac glorious, iris, tulips, golden basket. These blue gold days of spring I don't want to go away. Birds. Langorous feelings. Moments I sit out, and then I think I'm getting better, maybe have cheated the cancer-committee. I do hope so. There are so many lovely things to do and see. I'd like to write another book or two, or rather, to have written them. I'd like to see Terry and the family in smoother, sunnier weather, even though I know all weather's good for growth. This is easier to accept for oneself than for one's loves. Then the pain and the nausea return, especially in the "small" huge hours of the night, and I know I must wind up and set out for the rest of the Kelly treatment.

Friday, April 30th.

We don't often see the eagles these days, but when we do they are so unexpected and so intimate, soaring above the Pipes in different places, by the stream and down it, and now especially in a new place, a grove of oak trees at the very top of the road, down to the right, a peaceful place, but full of unseen awesome Presences, standing strongly by.

Tuesday, May 4th.

Iren's last concert of the season. Beautiful as always. A big crowd for the small space. Spring evenings have set in. The garden was overflowing with roses, lilac, especially the white lilac tree, where I smoke, lilies of the valley, and irises, irises everywhere. The flowers grow here so well because of Iren's music and her gardening hands.

> Earth's crammed with heaven,
> And every common bush afire with God,
> But only he who sees takes off his shoes.
> Elizabeth Barrett Browning

> Paracelsus tells us that if we knew all the qualities of the stars we would find that the "quality of each one of them is represented on earth by some plants. It is no inconsistent thing to say that every stone, flower, and tree has its horoscope."
>
> The group spirit of plants from its focus in the center of the earth, also emanates a spectrum of light which is absorbed by the roots of plants, carried up in the life force or sap, and used by nature spirits to color the plant kingdoms exactly in accordance with its varying development. Thus flowers truly "write music in the air proclaiming to all who observe them the position of their evolutionary status."[4]

The evolutionary status of our flowers must be excellent, thanks to the music and the love they get.

Thursday, May 6th.

Finished packing and got my will witnessed by Betty and the Health Department people. I had a car-

---

4. Corinne Heline, *Healing and Regeneration Through Color* (Los Angeles: New Age Press, 1979).

rot-juice mustache, I discovered later. What must they have thought? But instead of wheeling off in state this afternoon in Blue Miracle,[5] there was rain and wind and snow, and we couldn't leave. I was fretful over this, having already gone in my mind, and found the detachment from everything here painful, but there must be a good reason for the delay.

Friday, May 7th.

Still grounded by the weather, after a bad night. I called A. at the Hambidge Center and heard all was fixed for Aug. 15th to Sept. 30th. I felt guilty not warning them that I might have to cancel, if I need to. I wrote all the checks for bills that I had buried in a drawer and got that much ahead. I must say the last few weeks have been a very down time, in my lower self. The year of the Dragon doesn't seem to be my year. But there have been some good things, and good things lie ahead. The majestic Tai Ch'i teacher has told me I must pause on my journey northward and go to see a mystic spiritual healer in San Jose. This decided the direction we should start in, and that we would go up from there along the coast. I look forward to that encounter with the healing sea.

Saturday, May 8th.

We set off today, escorted by an eagle hawk and six crows. We saw the eagle again when we reached Yosemite. The weather was a marvelous turn-around from the last two stormy days. When we got to Tioga Pass it was open, but raining a little, then a lot, then

5. Edie called her dark blue camper Blue Miracle after my father's horse killed under him in France, 1916. It was the first horse I rode. I was put on his back when I was two.

snow. We went through awesome places. What contrasts! What cosmic messages! Stopped somewhere off the road in Bear country for Edie to sleep. She was sick this morning and yesterday, but driving all these miles valiantly, through unforgettable panorama. We loved it. At night we got to a strange little campground at Lake MacClure. It smelled awful but we stayed *quand meme*. Fortunately we had already smoked, in a little turn-off outside of Yosemite, on the eastern slope, a magic place, with a big rock to hide us, and the sort of little glades where the elementals live. I thought of Iren and Pommy. I was depressed when I left them this morning. I am easily emotionally upset these days, though I try to control it. Self-pity is a very stupid and infra-dig thing.

Sunday, May 9th.

We saw golden eagles several times and once again one swooped down very close and almost hugged me. We found a place by the river, full of birds and had breakfast there. Then we drove on and on and on, through interesting but depressing country, the Armour Empire, for example, miles and miles of it. Then on and on and on, over the mountains, much like the drive from Bakersfield to Walker Pass, and nowhere to smoke. Everything either had high fences or "No Trespassing" signs. One likely place we stopped, and a highway patrol man zoomed up to make us move on. He said it was a bad place, the body of a man murdered in Oakland was thrown into the ravine, from where we were. I would have liked to explain that this was all the more reason for us to bless the place with our Pipes, and help the spirit of the man if he was still earth-bound, to make his way from his discarded overcoat towards the light. We could also help to restore serenity to the nature spirits and the growing things, "all our relatives," there. These are the simple, fundamental needs which should be understood by all, but which, in our absurd set-up, can never be mentioned safely to authority—or indeed to almost anyone. We drove on, shepherded out by this kind officer. Finally we got to San Jose and went to the county park. We ate there but couldn't camp. So we went to a parking lot outside a big grocery store and tried to look like some delivery van, there for the night.

Monday, May 10th.

Woke to a gray day after strenuous dreams of enrolling in a rescue unit and being expected to do a solo flight in a small plane, without any training or even seeing it. All sorts of conversations, and decision not to do the flight, but to continue the commitment. Many people involved.

We got to Dr. G.'s house on the dot. I found myself quailing, hanging back. Our Joh Rei friend had said that this woman was "the nearest thing to an adept" that she had ever encountered. I did not feel up to an encounter with an adept, and yet was magnetically drawn forward. I rang the bell. After a little wait a small iron grille opened and an awesome personage looked out. It was a face I knew, but could not recognize until later. She led us in and placed me in a chair at right angles to hers, for a questioning period on all the planes. At the start of it she said "Now tell me about you." I said "About me? Or about the symptoms?" She smiled at the distinction. I began to feel more comfortably at home. The room in which we sat was a spacious oblong with a high old-fashioned ceiling. It was full of massive comfortable furniture and Buddhic treasures. My chair faced a fireplace,

and over it a bas-relief of a compassionate Boddhisat-
tva, or a Tibetan Goddess of mercy. She was flanked
by candlesticks and incense sticks, one of which was
lit and burning. One might expect to find the timeless
otherworld vibrations of such a room in a Tibetan
monastery, in the Himalayas. Later I learned that
many Tibetans and the Dalai Lama himself were patients of my adept.

After some more preliminaries she took me into
another room and had me lie down, then put some of
my saliva onto a tissue and fed it into a strange com-
puter-like instrument, marked "for diagnosis only."
After awhile she laid her healing hands on me and
gave me a treatment. We talked in snatches, getting
always nearer to each other's ch'i. She had been in
Rainbow D's sweat lodge, his wife a longtime patient
of hers. She knew Eagleman. She told me finally that
I had no new cancer but the old one had left traces,
adhesions, and damage to pancreas and liver. She
thought the cancer could be prevented from starting
up again.

Tuesday, May 11th.

Up early and drove to my adept with my Pipe. We
smoked in her living room in front of the fire, with
the statue above it. It was a good communion. The
rapport between us grows each time and I learned
more about her today. She gave me a very strong
treatment, and then said, "Go away and have fun." I
asked, "Who gives fun to you?" She said "You." We
had laughed together a lot. Then she said that she
liked to travel, especially in the East and was going
on a peace journey with some of her young people
and I think some Rinpochés and Lamas. She talked
about Eagleman. I got a new light on him, very help-

ful. Then we left, to go back to the Fairground where we are camping, all among the horses and gypsies.

Wednesday, May 12th.

My adept gave me another strong healing ending with her mantram. She told me many things today. I would not die of cancer, I would die of a stroke. I must discipline myself to write. My writing is my work, but I must also take care of those who come to me. I am starting a new cycle. The people who come will be new or will be growing higher. I am finishing up karma in this life with all sorts of people. I shall start next life free of these people and the karma. My ill health comes not from my mind but from wrong food. My power is in my hands, that is why I must write for myself and cannot dictate, etc. Some of these things I knew but it is wonderful to have them confirmed by such a great one. I suppose I should stop calling her adept since she denies it. I will call her Dr. G. Her information about Eagleman has been so right and so helpful. I left feeling very happy. Returned at 5:00 to meet her friends the Ks. Mrs. K. very sick with damaged lung. In spite of her husband's fear of smoke for her breathing, she begged for a healing Pipe. So we smoked on the patio, I trying to blow the smoke away from her, and the Grandfathers wrapping it all round her. Afterwards I used my stone and feather on her. She did begin to feel more comfortable and to breathe a little better. Then we went back to the Fairground.

Thursday, May 13th.

Up early and to Dr. G. Meditation with her most impressive and moving. Last treatment. She brings in the light almost palpably. Her hands are extraordinary. Then she drove us to San Mateo to a Buddhist Temple meeting, very interesting. I had not attended one since far-off Paris days, when I used to go to the Lotus Ceremony in the Musee Guimet. The Lama conducting it was Sister Palma, shaved head, robes, etc., an Englishwoman, long-time friend of Dr. G. She gave me a healing blessing. The disciples and young things round her were very earnest and devout, the ceremony, a puja, simple and good. Afterwards lunch on the lawn with the K.s, who were surprised to see me. Sister Palma joined us. I sat beside her and tried to comport myself as the Medicine Woman I was represented as being in spite of protests in private. I was abashed at being publicly introduced so but there it was. One does not contradict an adept. Sister Palma's accent and her amused smile told me much about her English background. I brought out a password or two from that long-forgotten life, and we were comfortably at ease together. A far cry for both of us from London life.

When we got back to Dr. G's house I told her that I felt there was no need to go on to the Kelly Institute, that I knew she had healed me. She said I must go just the same, must finish the pilgrimage, and get the nutritional counsel and abide by it. She gave us stern directions how to go and when. We obeyed and were wafted through San Francisco, on up Highway 1. Now it was cold and refreshing after the last few days of heat. We found a campground by the sea, smoked our Pipes under the huge full moon for the Wesak Festival, for which the Buddhist ceremonies today and tonight were held.

Friday, May 14th.

I slept the deepest sleep I have for months and woke a new person. The cells in my overcoat have understood what is right for them to do, have understood that I love them and they are busily healing themselves. I wonder why it takes so long to recognize that atoms and cells are sentient, puzzled beings, wondering why their existence seems to be ignored by us, for whom they toil at multitudinous tasks. I feel wonderfully well. Why wouldn't I? After so many healings. We made a late start after doing all sorts of chores which I enjoyed, and then sped on up the coast, an incredibly beautiful drive, wild flowers everywhere, all at their best, carpets of them, and the sea from every angle, rocks, spray, coves, every now and then a turn inland beneath great trees and shrubs in bloom, and then back to the sea. We had the Pipe on the edge of a cliff, all among wild lupins. These were the blue kind, but everywhere there have been yellow ones. Eventually we had to join Highway 101 and go inland, probably all tomorrow too, until we rejoin the sea at Eureka. But it is still beautiful and we are camped among the redwoods, in a good camp, with privacy and peace. We had an evening fire. I went to bed still feeling *well*, an unusual experience.

Saturday, May 15th.

We followed 101 through wild flowers, green ferns, etc. to the Avenue of the Great Redwood Trees. This was as awesome as it is always said to be. "Ye vastest Breathers of the Air" reminded us of the Ents in the Tolkien book. Later when we parked and slipped into a grove for the Pipe, the atmosphere was full of Presences and their strong vibrations, mysterious, chilling, harrowing the senses and the soul. We sat too near the road for the comfort of silence, but hidden behind a great tree with greater ones off to the side, vines and small flowers around them. A robin stayed on a branch of a lesser tree, opposite the smoking place, talking in low tones to us and to his family. I asked for him to be blessed and eventually he flew away. This would be a good place to bring my groups to for instruction. The trees would speak to them as they did to me.

Monday, May 17th.

We drove on round the Olympic peninsula which was disappointing, too overgrown to see the sea. Many showers, a gray depressing effect. The Indian village we looked forward to was nothing at all, a head-start group of mixed children, dancing to horrible whitey music of the worthless kind. Alas.

Wednesday, May 19th.

The great day of the tests. I don't know quite what I think. Dr. Kelly is a fanatic and perhaps a bit paranoid, with good reason. His computer, though on another plane from hers, seems to agree, in substance with Dr. G.'s, though he says I do have cancer in the lymph glands, but that it is slight and my basal metabolism is much better than most of his patients, though a lot of it, must be upped. I received a fat booklet full of guidelines and recipes for the new food. I think that since Dr. G.'s treatments and the Buddhist one I do not have cancer. Dr. Kelly was working from the answers I sent in a month ago before the other treatments. His instrument works with data and a drop of blood, hers with vibrations and spit. It's all rather fascinating and I wish that I didn't have a little cautionary imp saying—"are you sure?" But I am sure of several things, new things to think about, all recently brought to my attention by books, by Dr. G. and by this man. One thing, I am responsible for my own cells and can talk to them.

Friday, May 21st.

This is certainly unpolluted glorious country, mountains, wild flowers, the river. This is a paradise, unspoiled, gentle, awesome, happy. I loved it and all the enrichment my journey here has brought. Then, driving through Winthrop we heard that the whole area is doomed. Aspen has bought up acres and acres, sneakily, through private deals, to make a resort, skiers in winter, hordes in summer, and there it is, polluted, spoiled. I felt stricken, and the drive to the night's campground did nothing to lighten my sorrow, for we went by the sluggish waters of what used to be the Columbia river, dirty and low and ruined. The best spot I've found in recent years that still has the old kind of innocent, happy, unspoiled vibrations is due to be destroyed this December! I wish that I had been coming here all these years. Once doesn't seem to be enough. Before I knew about this encroachment I was praying that it might not be spoiled and might not be polluted. I probably picked up the anxieties of the nature spirits and the devas, and those angry, sensitive humans who later told us what would be happening.

Saturday, May 22nd.

Twice on the way my eagle-hawk appeared, dipped his wings, and my spirits soared again, but the drive was not so good, through sterile country farmed in the wrong way by big combines. Not a sign of life, here and there machines, but never a chicken (we were looking for good eggs) nor a dog, nor a cow. Later it got better, interesting around the Snake River with some lush parts, and later on the borders of Oregon some pines and streams. We camped in a fairly good place, not jammed, considering Saturday weekend near some towns, but oh so unlike where we have been. This place does its best but there are human vibrations everywhere, even though comparatively pleasant ones, and voices etc. We managed to have the Pipe by camouflaging one side with a chair and choosing a time when the community was fishing. Then we had a pleasant, quiet night. But I wish that it were possible to emerge openly with the Pipe and have everyone within the area join us, for a simple, natural, fundamental way of worshipping the Great Spirit and helping to heal our Mother Earth. Beer parties and raucous music and sex get-togethers are all acceptable, or seem to be understood, not so sitting in a sacred circle with the Pipe.

Sunday, May 23rd.

Stopped at a rawhide place where a friendly man gave us some scraps and sold us some better pieces. We gave him *Snowy Earth Comes Gliding* and bought two of his sister's poetry books, very sensitive work. She lives near an Indian reservation, which next time we will visit. This time doesn't seem to be an Indian pilgrimage. We went by a Paiute reservation near Burns, but didn't turn in. Saw some Paiutes by the wayside and didn't stop to speak to them as I would have done, before the old political hate-the-whites set in again. Talked this morning about healing stones and the mineral kingdom. I shall take that up with the group when I get back to them. It will help to develop their hands.

Monday, May 24th.

Blue Miracle rolled smoothly on. We had several glimpses of Grandfathers. We have come by beautiful roads through beautiful places, very few ugly spots, no traffic to speak of, especially on the back roads. It has been a good and happy trip. I have tried every day to communicate with the cells and atoms in my overcoat. A new idea to me. I had no real notion of this form of healing before this journey. Smoked by the stream a thanksgiving Pipe for all the blessings.

Thursday, May 27th.

Resting today, unpacking a little. I love my writing room, with all the books, and roses, masses of them, and I love my little sitting-room sanctum where I see my "patients." I began the three days purge, Epsom Salts three half hours apart, fruit juice to live on, weakness, and everything a sort of duty to one's atoms and cells, and a feeling of, I suppose, eventide. I am lucky that this came when I had money enough to cover it and no office job or responsibility for children. I also have had the experiences of healing and of Dr. G. telling me, which I instantly believed, that the cancer has gone, only the remaining damage left to deal with and the precancerous cells wanting to start up again, to be prevented.

Friday, May 28th.

Second day of purge. I do not mind it, even with people eating all around me. All that is difficult is the constant reminder of *why* and of the body. It is a strange thing to have had cancer. It sets one apart from others in a sort of way, and very far apart from oneself as one was before the knowledge of it surfaced.

Thursday, June 3rd.

I know how Paul felt as I go through all these contortions, enemas, and strange foods. My lymph glands are swollen, my back aches, I have gas and burps and everyone tells me these are not symptoms of the cancer, as they were before, but symptoms of the *cure!* It's an upside down situation, but I do believe my body is getting better, and I do believe in Dr. G. and her treatments and what she told me. This is just a bad quarter of an hour to get through, later—twenty months, Dr. Kelly said it would take—when I am well, it will have been worth it. Besides, I have no choice, the alternatives are too grim.

Friday, June 4th.

It's strange how karma works for me. Some day I expect I shall learn why. Perhaps if the breaks had gone the way they seemed to be surely going, I would have wasted the growth possible in this life for me, through the path I've traveled in pain, humiliation, loneliness and failure. If I had stayed a best seller, in New York, I might have needed several more lives to learn even the little I have absorbed in this oblivion. I like to think it may have been for that sort of reason. Here I am, out of the rat-race, in a beautiful place, with all my needs taken care of—*wants* are another thing and probably not good for us.

Saturday, June 5th.

I'm still thinking over the museum job and not coming to much of a conclusion. Some years ago I'd have leapt at it, but a seventy-three year-old, fighting cancer, with a book to write and another perhaps to follow, and a lodge and a group and patients—it seems a little unwise to take on anything else. I've been asking for the gift of discernment. Perhaps this is something to test it on.

When I reached this sort of low, out of touch with higher ranges, I took my Pipe and went alone to a place where there was peace. It was hard to find a time to be alone, and peace was harder still, but

when I could and did, the Grandfathers and Grandmothers accosted me, scolded me, shook me into balance and left me restored. Life took on a rhythm.
Every six weeks I drove across the mountains, or
rather I was driven, in Edie's Tioga camper, taking a
day and a night and a day, to adept Dr. G. Here there
were strenuous treatments, meditations in depth,
group meetings of many sorts, and interesting experiences. I usually stayed five days, until the cancer
count went down, which after a tussle, it did, reluc-
tantly. Then there would be a day or two of toxic,
swamping and nauseating me, and then I would feel
almost well for another space of time. The spaces
narrowed, six weeks, five weeks, a month, three
weeks. It made steady work on any book very difficult, but always these times with Dr. G. and her
group were memorable times, filled with flashing insights, and bringing in of Light.

Once I found a Lama there, a member of the Yellow Hat Order of the Dalai Lama, a friend and high-
ranking associate of His Holiness. He was accompanied by two monks, who cooked his food and attended to his needs. He did not come out of his bed-
room, but sat cross-legged on the bed, his head
against the window, so that the favored few allowed
to meet him and obtain his blessing could not see his
face, only the nimbus of light behind him.

One by one we climbed the stairs in our stockinged
feet, to kneel and answer questions put to us through
the interpreting monk. Many of the words the Geshe
used sounded to me like Navajo, and were spoken
with the same rhythmic inflections. He asked
through the interpreter what I wanted. I was clumsy
and uncertain, stupidly self-conscious. I asked him,
through the interpreter if he would bless my pipe and
my crystal. He took the pipe and put it on his lap and

clicked his beads around it. The sound startled me into a remembrance which was gone before I could catch it. He gave back the Pipe, took the crystal but did not click the rosary round it. He was silent. He seemed to be waiting for me to tell him something. After a struggle with my reluctance to talk, I told him that I had terminal cancer, and asked what I should do in the interval of waiting.

He answered, gently, always through the interpreter, "Do you practice Dharma?" I said "Not in the Buddhist way, perhaps, but yes, I try, in my own way." He asked if I had good motivation in healing? Was it to help people? I said, "Yes. What other motive could there be?" He said that was good dharma and I should practice good dharma. I thanked him and rose from kneeling to leave. I still couldn't see his face but I felt his strong, holy aura, and I felt his blessing. I was happy.

When I got back to my corner I continued to go over the experience. I meditated on the eightfold Buddhic way and the symbolic entrances to the center on my medicine wheel medallion, represented by eight stylized turtles. I thought that instead of stressing the conflicts and disagreements between nations, races, tribes, and people, instead of wanting everyone to be alike, we should give thanks that the Creator has created infinite diversity and individual uniqueness, that no two snowflakes are the same. We spend too much time trying to make a hummingbird behave like a bear. Both are power animals, both are Grandfathers, both work together in healing and ceremonies in perfect harmony. Neither is better or more right than the other. Certainly neither is the *only* right, has the *only* truth. We should approach all the divergencies as the French do the two sexes, crying delightedly "Vive la différence!"

Unique individual qualities are to be appreciated and cherished. More important is the unity behind them, all on the Medicine Wheel, all traveling toward the same Center; our Mother Earth and everything upon her, "all our relatives," evolving together toward the light. "For none may move alone upon the Spiral Way."[6]

Next day there was another foregathering. We were instructed by the interpreting monk in the method of "taking refuge." Then seven of us who were considered "healers" mounted the stairs again in our bare feet and were ushered into the Geshe's presence. He spoke about the ceremony and the reality of "taking refuge." Then we prostrated ourselves in the proper ways and times. This was difficult for me, not to get down, but to get up again, in my weakened state. We still could not see his face, as we repeated a very long mantram in Tibetan. Much of it sounded like Arapaho or Micmac. My Indian name sounded out often. "Taking refuge" the interpreter translated meant that we were included in Buddhic happenings, "such as the one Geshe Rampat expects in a month." (I never did discover who Geshe Rampat was, nor what the happening.) We will have a translation of the long mantram we have just said. Meanwhile we are to use the *Om Mani Padme Hum.* We each received a red ribbon after Geshe had breathed on it, for protection and awareness.

In the evening the Geshe came downstairs, and we got our first glimpse of his face. Again the likeness to the Navajo Medicine men struck me. He sat on an improvised throne near the fireplace and spoke to a larger group of Dr. G.'s students. His presence and

6. From *The Progression.* See End Notes on Joseph Wood.

the energy of his force field were more impressive than what he actually said through the interpreter. He was meeting us on a deeper level.

Several times when I came to be helped by Dr. G. there were other seers and teachers. Once she took me to a Sufi meeting where I was included in the sacred dance and received a blessing from the leader. In all these experiences I seemed to understand more clearly the universality of the Medicine Wheel and how it included all vision quests and all Shamanic and other journeys to the Center and Source of All. I also began to have intensive dreams more frequently, sometimes in sequences, and as my other-plane life stepped up, so did my this-plane life. I began to travel to different gatherings separated by race or creed or circumstance, between whom bridges should be made, and to do my share of the bridging.

It was Dr. G. who started me on this, first by encouraging me to speak to groups of her students, to include them in healing and other ceremonies with my Pipe, and generally to have more confidence in myself as a transmitting channel. It was from her house that I went to meet Oh Shinnah, the Apache Medicine Woman. I quote from the log-book:

"Our meeting with her was wonderful and important. She greeted us warmly. I offered her tobacco and *Snowy Earth Comes Gliding*, and asked for her blessing and counsel. She told me she had seen the tall Indian Guide who was with me, and she said she had prepared something for me and went to get it. It was a large healing crystal. She told me how to use it and gave me more healing advice and said I must have courage and if opposed by Indians or others, I was to say, "I'm doing this because you're not, and you should be!" I told her about the coming Oklahoma time[7] and she said it was important to give out now what we must share. She spoke of the coming purification and a lot of other things. Then she asked us to stay to bless a young mother near delivery and the coming baby. Her blessing was beautiful to watch and to share—the pollen, the feather, the advice."

Later Oh Shinnah asked me to be her adopted grandmother. She was one of the first of the sizable group of granddaughters and grandsons who call me "Gramma."[8]

During this period my path took on new patterns. I returned to Dr. G. in regular, more or less, cycles, first every six weeks, then every five weeks, then once a month, then I could stay away only for three weeks. Each time the "cancer count" had climbed high and each time the treatments brought it down. These four or five days of meditation, of "bringing in the Great White Light of Healing," of exercises and vibrations, and exposure to many other measures and methods, kept my human envelope going long after its medically allotted time, long after any logical time for me to stay with it. It was as though the Grandfathers and Those Above were saying, "there's some more mileage in this old jalopy. Keep her going. She's dumb but she's willing, and we need all the willing helpers we can get."

Between treatments I traveled over a large part of the West, and as far east as Georgia and Texas. I even went to England, briefly to finish up some family karma there and find the ley lines to some Power Places. Wherever I went was for short, intensive periods of work within different groups. I spoke on the Pipe, the Medicine Wheel, the Sun Dance, the Native

---

7. Part of an extended tour in 1978, which I was dreading.
8. I am official Grandmother to N.A.M.A. and to many others.

American ways of life; I took part in Medicine Wheel gatherings, I attended a Sun Dance in Montana and "stood behind," i.e. gave support to, two dancers, as their adopted Grandmother. I also wrote books and articles, and took care of the people who came to me for training or for help with problems.

During the journeying that followed and the jottings of the log-book inadequately describing it, I seemed to be swinging on a powerful pendulum between invading cancers attacking many parts of my human envelope and miraculous remissions when my body was clean and freed from these intrusions, leaving occupied territory damaged and energies weakened.

Gradually I learned how to pass through these "terminal" times, when I approached the entrance to the Tunnel, without knowing whether I would go further or emerge from it, into the troughs between the swings. The Tunnel and the entrance to it were familiar to me now.

Sunday, July 24th, 1977.

I felt a little émotionnée at the Pipe this morning, and for the last few days have also been fighting tears. I hope not of self-pity. I have been trying to come to terms with this shortening of the cycle for some time, and to set things straight to leave as little burden behind as possible.

More and more I feel as though I were in a play, one of Dr. Elizabeth Kubler Ross's case histories like those of the play Shadow Box—in which Terry played the part of the daughter of the dying woman, an odd experience for me in the audience, and for her on the stage. However well prepared I have been by so many wise people, it still comes as a strange shock each time. This time Dr. G. asked "How long does it take you to write a book?" When I said, "with all the research done, about two years." She said, "Don't start one." So I don't need to write another, can't in fact, finish this one,[9] and must set my house in order again.

We drove out to the Catholic sisters Aspasia[10] had told me I could help. I was prepared for the formality of the "habit," but I found them in shorts and blue jeans. There was an instant bridge between us. I heard their problems and asked for their way to be made clear to them. It was odd to walk into a Dominican group of nuns and quite naturally, at this first meeting, sit them down under the redwood trees for an Indian Pipe. I liked them so much and all that they are doing. It is strange to be on the way out instead of the way into this group—so many lovely people in the world and I am only just finding them. But I will be given the grace I need to go through whatever is allotted to me now.

Friday, July 28th.

I dreamed tonight of a lot of confusing work among people and of sitting on a high place in a garden, with a young man beside me. He was fair and young and cleanshaven, and he was consulting me whether he should say yes or no to a job, a priestly job, for he was a young priest. I told him some of the benefits, a little house, a chapel, and the power to help many people. Then I leaned forward and said impressively, "You see, this is the Scattered Brotherhood." It startled me to say it, and hear it said, but I

---

9. *I Send A Voice,* which did get finished and was published by Quest Books in 1978.
10. Aspasia Voulis. See End Notes.

knew it was true. Then I modified it, saying "It is the kindergarten for the Scattered Brotherhood."

Saturday, July 29th.

This night I had a dream that I was with people at a sort of crowded concert hall, in the gallery, with Iren playing out of the confusion below. Suddenly she seemed to be with us in the gallery, and she was singing in a deep rich contralto, ending in a cough. She said "My voice isn't strong," but she was singing very strongly until she coughed, and she was singing a popular melody, warm and human. There followed my usual dream of a big building with floors and elevators and complications, and my trying to find my room there. I know parts of that building very well and the various dining rooms on some floors, and the outside streets leading to it. When I woke I felt that Iren had been singing "the last song" for me, and that it *was* more mellow and warm and human now.

I had a moment of self-pity or something with my morning Pipe. It passed in the smoking. I am serene and full of joy. Uncertainty is a strain, but I am acting on the assumption that it is a question of a few months. Then if it proves longer my affairs will be in order and I shall be more free to continue working here. I may feel a little foolish, like Lazarus when he had to go back to the office, but so what?

Wednesday, August 2nd.

These days I am full of the sweetness of life and tenderness towards Mother Earth. I love Her. As I write I see the tall mountain with the icecap on her head and the silhouette against a golden ivory light. Our jungle of a garden hides us completely. Now and then I have to try not to cry. I don't think it's self-pity.

I think it's just so much that I didn't do, didn't see, and cannot now embark upon. I think it's partly love for brave, poor humans, most of us sick and disappointed in our this-plane lives—nothing turning out just right. Except God. And Sometimes it's hard to realize that He-She is vulnerable too and growing. Even the Source of all compassion is not static.

Thursday, August 3rd.

I feel wambly today, weak in the legs, but not in too much pain. I rested more than usual. I went into the Guru bath as usual. This is an old-fashioned horse trough set up in the garden behind trellises. It is particularly refreshing this summer. Everyone should have a round horse trough and a private place to put it. Ours is just right. As a meditation and a place for healing it is very powerful.

Sunday, August 10th.

The wedding of two of Dr. G.'s group. She had asked me to assist her in marrying them. First we smoked the Pipe in the center of the circle where the young people will dance, and we decided on the exact spot for the wedding, a circle of great trees round a large open place. It was a lovely wedding. We began it with Smudging. I spoke before the exchange of rings, then Dr. G. married them, with a simple exchange of what they wanted to say to each other. After the blessing we collected them into a circle around the bride and groom and we all danced, an Indian step I showed them. Then the newly married couple greeted everyone and went off to a wedding lunch under the trees.

Monday, August 21st.

We drove to the Dominican sisters, and had another good meeting with them. As we were smoking

beneath their redwoods came the high clear call of a
great bird, like the Eagle-bone whistle, far above. It
reminded me of a vision B. had at one of my workshops. He drew me aside to tell me that he saw me in
front of a table facing him. On the table there was an
open book, with the pages fluttering back and forth
in a stirring of air. I was saying, "I can't do it." Then
a great white bird came flying from behind me. It settled on my shoulders, or just back of me, and began
as B. said, "to rough up my head with its beak." A
voice, either from the bird or from behind it said,
"You *can* do it. You are as you are. Don't fail that."
Then his vision faded. I was startled. The next day, a
correspondent on the other side of Turtle Island,
who lived with a medium for White Eagle, sent me a
message saying: "Yes, it is so. Your White Eagle is indeed our White Eagle, and the books are his also.[11]
He has asked me to say that he is happy to be able to
work through you, that you are a good instrument
and have a lot of power. He sends you his blessing
for the coming year." Without this message I might
have thought that B.'s "great white bird" was the
Whistling Swan accompanying my Pipe. Either way
it would be a great blessing.

🔲🔲🔲🔲

The next log book entries are full of pain and discomfort, and Dr. G. cancelling a trip to India to be with
me, and her group getting ready to waft me through
the Tunnel. Naturally, when we were keyed up for
my departure, there came another miraculous remission. I felt the group's disappointment (and my own
a little too). I said "Now I've lost all my glamor," and
they laughed. Dr. G. knows I am ready to go or to
stay. She feels there is something more for me to do.

---

11. White Eagle. See End Notes.

Probably, or I would have gone when so many expected me to take off the overcoat they had worked hard to keep around me.

Everyone is "terminal," or rather, all our overcoats are terminal. The only difference between one termination and another is that some of us are warned of the drawing near of the launching and some are not. Even when we're warned and ready (more or less) for the blastoff, it may not take place as scheduled, or it may come sooner, or be scrubbed, and another, different mission set up. The only certainty is that the transition comes for us all. I don't believe it would be helpful to continue with descriptions of the ups and downs, onslaughts and remissions, of the next years to the present. Through them all I was learning, as were others, valuable insights and priorities upon the Way. Through them all I was used as a channel to transmit light and healing from Those Above to those who were sent to me to give help, to receive it.

I was becoming more and more aware of life in the round, of living the circle, and of the eternally repeated time-cycle. And I began to have intimations in dreams, meditations and happenings, of the Shamanic journey in the Spirit Canoe.

Now began a period of traveling and public appearances between the healing sessions. Instead of private appearances at small gatherings, I found myself drawn into public gatherings of several hundred people. One of the most significant of these came about in November, 1979. I was invited at the last moment to be a participant, "a presenter," at the Symposium, "The Seventh Arrow," built about Hyemeyohst Storm's great classic Seven Arrows.

"The Seventh of these arrows is the Harmony which holds all things together."[12]

Wednesday, November 7th.

We started off in good time and we had a wonderful traveling day, through the mountains, aspen trees in streams down the mountainsides and snow in patches. Here we are on a long mission. I don't feel well prepared but I'm not nervous, knowing that if I stay channelled the right words and actions will come through. We spent the next day going down the Sacramento River towards Berkeley. Amazing that one can travel this unexplored (to us) and very little driven region paralleling the great highways and freeways that are so taxing—in the peace of river banks, levees and wildlife, with pheasants scuttling everywhere. We smoked on the riverbank, protected by Tioga from the rare passing car.

The Symposium was given in support of the "Healing of Schizophrenia, The Wholeness of Modern Man and the Recovery of the Sacred Dimension." It was presented by St. George Homes, Dorothea Romankiw's "Jungian, Transpersonal, New Age Residential Treatment Center for Schizophrenic and Autistic Adolescents." When I saw this I thought of Paul Nordoff's St. George's Home in England and wondered if they were connected. It was cosponsored by Fantasy Films,[13] The Department of Education, and the Committee for Arts and Letters of the University of California in Berkeley.

"This Symposium" the program explained "will be a living Medicine Wheel of Film, Mythic Drama,

---

12. Hyemeyohst Storm, *Seven Arrows* (New York: Harper and Row, 1975).

13. Fantasy Films, makers of *One Flew Over the Cuckoo's Nest, Three Warriors,* and *Lord of the Ring.*

Ceremony, Ritual, Lectures and Panel Discussions: a Vision Quest, to explore in-depth the new psychological insights to be gained from ancient Symbolic Traditions; a Teaching to demonstrate the central importance and transformative power of the archetypes in the healing of adolescent schizophrenia; a Balancing, to reaffirm the relevance of the Sacred Dimension to modern man's quest for Wholeness; a Festival and a Sharing."

It was all of those. It took place in the big Wheeler Auditorium. I discovered that I was expected to open and close each session. I decided that the best way to do this would be to use the traditional "smudging," which I explained and demonstrated. Then, since there were several of my students among the audience, I sent them with shells of burning sage down the aisles, so that those who wished could smudge themselves with the incense.

The smoke mushroomed up to the roof. Someone said to one of the smudgers, who repeated it to me, "What a strange idea to cleanse with smoke—but it worked. One could feel the difference right away." An aware one can, and this was a very "with it" audience.

The first program was to the South, the Direction of Trust and Openness. "The South is a time for the Water to run Freely. The Whole World becomes green."

The second was to the North, the Direction of Wisdom and Insight. "To the North on the Medicine Wheel is found Wisdom. The color of the Wisdom of the North is White, and its Medicine Animal is the Buffalo."

The third was to the West, the Direction of Reflection and Introspection. "The West is the place of looking within. When one looks within, he is able to Recognize the Stars that Guide him in his Times of darkness."[14]

During this third section the film *Three Warriors* was shown, a haunting, unforgettable movie. For many it was the high point of the Symposium, an impressive film about a troubled urban Native American who returns to the reservation. There he is taught the ancient ways of his people by his dignified, wise grandfather. He goes through a series of testing quests as he learns the meaning of being a true "Warrior." Slowly his views of himself and others and the urban life to which he must return, undergo transformation. But this gives no real idea of the impact of the film, the incredible photography, the eagle, the horse whose name is Three Warriors, the performances of all the cast and Sy Gomberg's moving account of how he came to write the script. It was appropriate to show this example of reflection and introspection during the section honoring the West. "The West is the place of looking within . . ." *Three Warriors* should be an essential part of passage rites for everyone. It should be shown yearly to schools.

The fourth section honored the East, the Direction of Illumination. "The place of the East is the way of total illumination. . . . The East begins the New Day for Man . . . the East is marked by the sign of the Eagle. It is the place of illumination where we can see things clearly, far and wide. Its color is the Gold of the Morning Sun."[15]

On the next and last day we honored Mother Earth

14. Storm, *Seven Arrows*.
15. Ibid.

and Father Sky. There was a Give-away. It fell to me to introduce and to explain it. I quoted from *The Gospel of the Redman:*

> Be not greedy of great riches. It is a shame and a disgrace of all unworthiness in a man to have great possessions when there are those of his tribe who are in want. When, by chance of war or of commerce, or the gifts of the Great Spirit that have blessed him with power, he has more than he has need of for himself and his family, he should call the people together and give a Potlatch or Feast of Giving, and distribute his surplus to those who have need, according to their need, especially remembering the widow, the orphan, and the helpless.[16]

Black Elk describes such a potlatch. Incidentally, potlatch is probably the origin of potluck.

> There was much giving away. It was time for the Sun Dance and the hearts of the people were strong. Our relatives gave horses to many, showing their gladness for our safe return; and the four of us gave and gave, until we had left only the horses we had before. If there had been more, we would have given them too; for the heart grows stronger with giving.

On another occasion he says:

> While the people were watching and eating, the relatives of the dancers were giving away many things—horses and fine clothing, beaded work and maybe tipis; for giving is a sacred deed and is pleasing to the Mysterious One Who gives everything.[17]

---

16. Ernest Thompson Seton, *The Gospel of the Redman* (Santa Fe: Seton Village, 1973).

17. John G. Neihard, *When the Tree Flowered* (New York: Simon and Schuster, Pocket Books, 1973).

A missionary to the Paiutes complained in the early eighteen hundreds that he despaired "of bringing them into civilization because they had no idea of selfishness and persisted in sharing everything they had." Apparently he said it seriously.

I was thinking of this as I told the audience about a Powwow I attended, sponsored by three small tribes working together, the Sac, the Fox, and the Ponca. It was an annual event, a Give-Away honoring those who had done something special for their tribes during the year. The dancers and some of the onlookers were wearing shawls with fringes, beautiful shawls, some of them fine "museum pieces."

As the drumming and the singing began and the dancers moved into the circle, their shawls filled the rather drab hall with tapestries of rainbow light. When the first dance ended, the dancers crossed the room and presented the shawls they wore to others. A woman next to me was given one. She took it and when the dancing began again entered the circle and danced for awhile, then left it and gave her shawl to another who danced for awhile and left to give away the shawl, and so it went, a continual exchange of beautiful shawls.

A little girl of perhaps ten years old had evidently done something good for her tribe that year, because she was presented with a magnificent red and gold shawl. She stood up triumphantly and ran into the circle. Here she danced her great moment of honor and recognition, joy in every inch of her, then she looked around her, thoughtfully, wistfully. We could see she still delighted in her shawl and wanted to dance longer, but she left the circle and went to where an older woman sat, perhaps her grandmother, and gave the shawl to her. This Elder was lame and hobbled with a stick, but she entered the circle and did a few steps—she must have been a good dancer earlier in life, she was bobbing rhythmically up and down. Then she gave the shawl to a young man and sat down.

There were some stars among the dancers who ended with several shawls presented to them, but only one to keep, the rest to give away. One girl was careless and let hers trail onto the floor. An older girl took it from her and gave it to someone else. This taking back a gift improperly cared for and giving it to someone else to use rightly may be the origin of the idea of "Indian Giving," not quite understood by whites. Gratitude and right use are essential to accepting gifts.

Before the last dance there was a Give-Away of lengths of cloth, groceries and other items. Then everyone in the room was invited into the circle. Those of us who had received cloths made improvised shawls of them, covering arms and shoulders, and danced behind the regular dancers. I thought as I bobbed up and down in the cloth I had received, "What a good way to teach the right way to deal with our possessions! Earn them, enjoy them, use them to the full, and give them away while you still love them."

Greed was discouraged and is still discouraged by those who follow the old ways. Outdoing the neighbors and having vast possessions was the way to get yourself thrown out of the tribe. Ownership was limited to what a family really needed and really used. Trade was carried on through barter by sticks or counters. On the Plains the smallest unit was an arrow, the next a beaver skin, the next a buffalo robe, then a horse with the value of two robes. In the east shell or wampum was used. There was no hoarding, because barter was usually completed at once.

We cannot go back to horses, buffalo, wampum, shells or the simplicities of direct barter, though some people are trying to revive that, but we could go forward to the philosophy behind the ancient ways of dealing with possessions.

Ernest Thompson Seton quotes in *Fundamental Laws:*

> No man owns land. A man owns only so much land as he tills or occupies with his house or his field. When he ceases to occupy that land, it goes back to the tribe, to be allotted to another member. No man owns the wood of the forest, or the water of the rivers, or the soil of the earth. He did not make them, they are the harvest of the land that belongs to the whole people; and only so much of them is his as he can gather with his own hands and use in his own house.[18]

Now that we parcel out the air above us and the sea around us into national territories, to say nothing of what we have done and are doing to our Mother Earth, we had better hold on to our shawls of achievement pretty tightly, lest they be taken from us and given to others, perhaps another species altogether, to use better. Or, a wild thought—remember the question "what if they gave a war and nobody came?" What if they gave a Powwow, a world-wide sharing Potlatch and *everybody* came?

The Give-Away at the symposium was especially moving. It consisted of baskets filled with treasures, cones, pieces of wood, pebbles, which the sick "children" had gathered during their summer campings, a reminder that those who seemingly have the least sometimes give the most generously of what they have. Another such reminder came from Jim Ham-

---

18. Seton, *Gospel of the Redman.*

mitt, the editor of *Mainstream*, a magazine for the physically handicapped. Jim's acknowledged brilliance of mind is encased in a human envelope of cerebral palsy. He came triumphantly struggling up the long center aisle to make his offering of three hundred copies of the magazine as a Give-Away from the Able-disabled to the Mentally disabled, who themselves were giving away to the rest of us.

I asked the audience to stand and make their own Give-Away. I used part of a prayer from a Pipe Ceremony: "Here I offer and present to you, Wakan Tanka,—(this Pipe and with it)—myself, all that I am, all that I shall be when I soar shining. Uniting with our relatives throughout the worlds which You have made, and all here present, I say Yes, Yes, Yes, *Yes!* to Your Divine Will for us and for all that You have made."[19]

The Yesses roared out and went soaring to the rafters, and beyond them. Then came the ceremony of Mother Earth. "We are part fire and part dream. We are the mirroring of Meaheyyum the total universe, upon this earth, our Mother. We are here to experience. We are a movement of a hand within millions and millions of sun fires. And we speak with the mirroring of the Sun."[20]

Later came the honoring of Father Sky, the Realm of Dreams. "Father Sky is the place dreams come from. Over-all the Sky is the power of the Vision and for the people on earth the power comes through dreams."[21]

Last came the ceremony of the Seventh Arrow and the recovery of the Sacred Dimension. "Each Man, Woman and Child upon the Earth is a living fire of

19. Wakan-Tanka, Source of All.
20. Storm, *Seven Arrows.*
21. M. Thor.

Power and Color . . . They are a living, Spinning Fire, a Medicine Wheel. And these colors from this living Wheel of Fire can be seen by all Men and Each Can Learn From Them."[22]

After the final panel discussion, with its summary of the shared experience, drama, progression, the Symposium came to a graceful conclusion. It fell to me to bless and dismiss the audience, as I had closed all the sessions, but this time with a Buddhic blessing, to emphasize the ecumenical nature of the occasion.

Hyemeyohst invited me to the Sun Dance to be held the next summer in Montana and asked me to be the Grandmother "standing behind" a young man who would be one of the dancers. Then we all dispersed.

Monday, November 12th, 1979.

We went to the St. George Homes for a visit with the schizophrenic "children," at the invitation of Dorothea Romankiw, the enlightened and extraordinary Founder of the Homes. My mind was still full of the experience of the Symposium. I was thinking of the Give-Away, and of Jim Hammitt's demonstration that the Able-disabled have empathy, sometimes a deep empathy, with the mentally disabled. Who would not choose a handicapped body housing a normal, and in his case a brilliant, mind, rather than a physically strong, often handsome body housing a brain-damaged mind? Here we were to see—alas, how hard it would be to *meet*—those able to suffer but unable to understand that suffering, unable to relate to the world in which their bodies exist, except by moments, except by miracles.

---

22. Storm, *Seven Arrows.*

Such moments and miracles do occur and have a poignancy, an almost unbearable impact upon lay-people who witness them, but hopeful and rewarding to the dedicated personnel who work with and live for the mentally disabled. We were to live through such a moment, such a miracle.

When we arrived, Hyemeyohst and his assistant Andrea were already there. Andrea was at the piano, playing to a roomful of young people, sitting or lying on brightly colored cushions, or wandering about the well-lit, attractive room, with attendants obviously warmly concerned, always near them.

"This is about an eagle," Andrea said. "I wrote it myself and came here to play it to you."

A few faces turned toward her, but most of the "children" went on blankly with whatever they were doing, walking, turning in circles, lying face downwards on cushions, making swimming motions, or staring at the walls.

I was sitting between Dorothea Romankiw and Hyemeyohst. At our feet, on a brilliant turquoise cushion, an oblivious young-old man rocked back and forth, back and forth, sometimes paddling with his hands, sometimes nodding rhythmically, always staring forward.

"He's going on a long, long journey," Hyemeyohst said.

I hoped it might be so, and not an expression of un-bearable pain in hopeless solitude. Whatever it was, he was lost in it. But perhaps even in these depths, far down the Cosmic Ladder, there might be a rope ladder to a spirit lifeboat and helpers reaching from it to pull the drowning up. Beside him a fair good-looking boy, more likely man, he could have been any age in the twenties, sat staring at us, and then at the pianist and then back to us. He was smiling a sweet, fixed smile. His eyes were blank. No one looked out of them.

"Andrea is going to make an eagle for us, flying over the mountain," Hyemeyohst said, and an attendant added, "Let's listen and see if we can see the eagle."

A few of the circle on the cushions seemed to be listening, but most of them continued in their separate worlds. When the music ended the attendants applauded and some of the children followed their example. Suddenly the man near us, I will call him Jim, clapped his hands together and said delightedly, "She did it!" He looked at us, and now his eyes were full of intelligence. Dorothea Romankiw beside me murmured, "A breakthrough!" She signed to Andrea to continue playing.

We could see Jim listening with full attention, and when she finished this time he said "She did it again!" The attendant behind him put his hand upon Jim's shoulder and Jim put up his hand in answer. I looked at Dorothea. She was smiling, but there was a mistiness in her eyes. I could see that this was a great moment, long waited for. Before I could follow it further the time had come for a circle of goodbyes. Everyone joined hands and there was a simple ceremony of thanksgiving. Then the "children" went away, shepherded by their attendants. Two women pulled the rocking man to his feet and held him kindly as they led him after the others.

Jim kept turning round to smile and wave at us. Hyemeyohst was deeply moved. "Beautiful!" he said to Dorothea as he waved to Jim and to the others. "Will it last?"

"I don't know," she said. "We hope so. It's a beginning."

Hyemeyohst's interest in the St. George Homes

(and mine) had been roused by the fact that Amerindian traditions and healing ways form part of the training treatment here. In the summers the "children" are taken into the country for intensive wilderness camping, including living in tipis and using simple rituals to develop rhythm and harmony with the Earth Mother. "Holistic and pragmatic" the flyer explains, and though primarily oriented to Carl Jung, there are many other approaches, a "resistance to closure. Whatever has not been demonstrated to fail is still possible."

I was asked to stay and meet more of the staff and speak to them about the way of the Pipe. I did so and then I invited them to smoke with me for the work of the Home, the "children" and those who ministered to them, that they might be strengthened and re-fueled. It was a very strong, high Pipe. One woman said after the first puff she went into another dimension and others were obviously moved. I blessed them, answered more questions, and then we left.

囗囗囗囗

I came away from this visit to the Bay Area with new vistas, intuitions, deeper awarenesses. One of the most important was meeting Hyemeyohst Storm. I had read, studied and taught his *Seven Arrows* for some years. The image I had built of him was that of a traditional Elder, a quiet, wise, awesome authority, much like Black Elk. I was not prepared for a stocky, younger man, with fair hair and blue eyes, whose way of speaking, unless he was dealing directly with sacred subjects was international man-of-the-world. He is Cheyenne, Crow, and German. I give thanks to Wakan Tanka that he is of this mixed heritage, and not confined to one strain only. It has made possible his great vision of N.A.M.A. (National American Métis Association).

Métis is a French word meaning Mixed. In the brochure explaining this to new people—it is wider than a tribe or a nation—Hyemeyohst says:

I am a Native born person—meaning that I was born in America. While I was a small child I did not feel the pains of being "a breed," but as I grew older I felt its bitter sting. I was an American who was alone. I am no longer alone because now I belong to the Métis people. Racists and separatists segregate Americans into "ethnic and racial groups." What do people do if they do not "fit" so conveniently into one of these "racial groups"? Well, I can tell you—they are alone.

There are millions of children and adult Americans who are of a "mixed blood." Then he or she is a Métis. A few hundred years ago everybody was an immigrant to America except for the "Indians," but those days are long gone. Anyone who says that Americans are of "European Roots" these days is a bit out of touch with reality and America. My ROOTS are America.

The estimated number of people in America who possess "a small degree of Indian blood" are twenty million. That's a lot of Métis. But a Métis is not just a person with Indian blood. Most Americans are such a mixture when they are asked about their "blood" they simply shrug their shoulders and reply that they are "full blooded Americans." A Métis is a "full blooded American."

The Métis do not try to find their heart and Roots by "going back in time." Why should we "go back"? What we are and what we need is right here. I have seen Métis people not "black enough" to belong to the Blacks, "red enough" to belong to the Indians, "white enough" to belong to the Whites or "yellow enough" to belong to the

Asians. I have seen tears, confusion and heart break.

Dry those tears, my Métis! You are a Métis!

You can wear feathers if you want to, play congo drums if you choose, wear leden hosen if you care to, or fly a Chinese kite.

The bigots may laugh at us, the racists may yell at us, the separatists may scream at us or the segregationists may curse us—but it does not matter —we are the Métis. We have Métis Medicine Men and Women who will teach us, we have our Present and our Past, we have our Sweet Land and we have one another; what else do we need?

I have little else to say beyond these words because Nama is your Good Circle. What else will be said about the Métis we will all say together. Join with us Métis People. Let us enjoy one another and work together to free America from its racists' ideologies.

Your Métis brother, Hyemeyohst Storm.

This is the vision Sun Bear[23] has, and before him Black Eagle, Wovoka and others, and many Channels and Seers spread over the earth. Sun Bear says:

In this vision I saw that the time drew near when, for the sake of the Earth Mother and all of our evolution as human beings, we must return to a better and truer understanding of the earth and all of our relations on her. I saw that we would have to put aside the petty fears that divided us and learn to live as true brothers and sisters in a loving way. I saw that we would have to find others who shared our heart's direction, whatever their racial background, and join with them into groups that always remembered that our purpose was to be instruments of the Great Spirit's will and helpers to our Earth Mother. I saw that such groups could

---

23. Sun Bear. See End Notes.

greatly effect the cleansing of the earth that is now occurring.

This was the part of my major vision that I can share at this time. Since the time that I had it I have been striving to fulfill it, with good results. I am the medicine chief of the Bear Tribe, a multiracial medicine society based upon that vision, and we reach many people with the work that we do and with the message that we have been entrusted to carry. Our message can be summed up in the phrase "Walk in Balance on the Earth Mother." This reflects all the attitudes of my people, a people who felt that their lives had to blend with all the things around and within them. They felt, as we do, that we have to come to a point when we truly feel the oneness, the unity, that connects us to all of the universe, and that we have to reflect that unity in all the aspects of our lives.

The rediscovery of the Medicine Wheel across Turtle Island and in parts of Europe, is one of the more hopeful developments of our difficult passage into the new era. As the Medicine Men and Women gather and their people round them, to work together and to complement and support each other in spreading the vision, and more important, *living* it, a new wind sweeps through the world. It may yet bring to birth the age-old dream of the Brotherhood of Man, the completed family of *all* our relatives upon the planet and perhaps one day beyond Her.

As David Spangler, writing about Findhorn says:

> They [people who think of Findhorn as if it were an isolated expression] are not aware of what is becoming a worldwide transformation, and that individuals in every country of this world and every walk of life are pursuing essentially the same vision. . . . We stand at the threshold of having developed enough awareness that humanity

shares a transcendent potential, and that perhaps we can learn to build a society and live a life attuned to its essence. This is the challenge of our time: to enter into a new consciousness which can, in turn, give birth to a new world.

The vision of an emergent planetary culture involves the broadening and deepening of our individual and collective perspectives and assumptions so that we embrace ourselves as a species, as humankind, rather than as separate factions. It involves, moreover, seeing ourselves as sensitive, interdependent members of a community of life that transcends the human and embraces the whole of planetary ecology, including the Earth itself as a living being. It is not seeing ourselves only as Eastern or Western, American, British, Russian, Chinese, African, or Asian. It is the rediscovery of our shared species identity that unites us beyond our national, racial, religious, economic and political boundaries.

Today, throughout the world, millions of people are consciously working with this vision. . . . In so doing they are becoming images and image-makers of a new culture, which is also, in its essential roots, the oldest and only culture there has ever been.[24]

This is the vision of the Metis and of the Medicine Wheel. Wherever people are exposed to it there is an explosion of joy, a visible transformation of the expression on people's faces and a lasting breakthrough of new energies directed to the healing of the Earth Mother.

🔲🔲🔲🔲

In the spring of 1980 we became neighbors of Sun Bear, Wabun and the Bear Medicine Tribe, through

24. David Spangler, *Revelations: The Birth of a New Age* (Elgin: Lorian Press, 1979).

the purchase of a piece of land abutting theirs, where they wanted to have like-minded people. This Mount Vision land, for a part of which we are custodians, is to be kept "undeveloped," in its natural state, as a center for ceremonies, vision quests, fasts, Sweat Lodges and other healing rites. Tipis, campers and a communal cook house occupy the bottom outer edge, leaving the boulder-studded, tree-covered slopes at the top undisturbed by intrusion.

Here we laid out a Medicine Wheel, which never has to be taken away, but remains pulsating light and energy to those within reach, a wide reach with no limits of time, distance, space. Here we come for re-fueling, refreshment and peace. Here Sun Bear invites us to his Sweat Lodge and Medicine Wheel, and we include the Bear Tribe and the strangers within their gates to any gathering of ours. It is a new-era relationship of two communities separate but really equal and together.

During the first two summers we held Pipe Ceremonies, Medicine Wheel Ceremonies and put several people into fast. We held our annual Council meeting in the Council Tipi. We blessed the boundaries, the great guardian rocks, the sacred trees. Then we had to leave physically to return to our various outposts, but we remain in unbroken touch with Mount Vision and often ascend there in our travel bodies. Others consider it their spiritual powerhouse, without being able to get there physically. Many are tithing to support its needs. No one can own land, bits of our Mother Earth, but it is theirs to protect and care for. It is theirs through unpossessive love.

In the summer of 1980 we set out for the Sun Dance to which Hyemeyohst Storm directed me to go, recommending me to Tom Yellowtail, the Crow Medicine Man who would be officiating.

Black Elk has said of the Sun Dance

> The Wiyag Wachipipi (dance looking at the Sun) is
> one of our greatest rites and was first held many
> many winters after our people received the sacred
> Pipe from the White Buffalo Cow Woman. It is
> held each year during the Moon of Fattening
> (June) or the Moon of Cherries Blackening (July)
> always at the same time when the moon is full, for
> the growing and dying of the moon reminds us of
> our ignorance which comes and goes; but when
> the moon is full it is as if the eternal light of the
> Great Spirit were upon the whole world.

He also said: "The Sun Dancers put rabbit skins on
their arms and legs, for the rabbit represents humility, because he is quiet and soft and not self-asserting
—a quality which we must all possess when we go to
the center of the world."

Before leaving home I put out the customary offerings for the grandson I was to support as he danced,
a complete meal, with other gifts and prayers, in a
high rocky place where eagles and other Grandparents are often seen.

Then I began some wind-up ceremonies with the
group and some preparations for the journey. It was
to be in three stages, a check-up and treatment from
Dr. G., a seminar at the Quaker Center in Ben Lo-
mond, which I was to conduct for a group of Catholic sisters, and then the trek to Montana.

Friday, June 13th, 1980.

Mt. St. Helen erupted again last night and covered
the Portland area with ashes. Not so big an eruption
as the first time, but more than the second. The Bear
Tribe say there has been no damage at Mount Vision.
They seem to think the ashes will be excellent topsoil
and fertilizer.

We started tonight on the vision quest for the group. We went first for a purification swim in Manzanar old reservoir. It was very full and we had it to ourselves. Icy cold, refreshing. Then to the place behind and above the great rocks of the theater site. Here we laid out a Medicine Wheel, danced, chanted, smoked our Pipes, each in place around the Wheel, and started our meditation as the dark fell. The stars came out and made a Medicine Wheel in the sky, above ours. After a long vigil Peggy played the flute, Kathy the drum, Judy spoke, Edie sang. Then we "went" into the center. After awhile we lay down in our sleeping bags and watched the Cosmic Wheel turning. Peggy sang through the night. It was very cold. At dawn we smoked the Pipes.

Saturday, June 14th.

After dawn Pipes we wandered for an hour among those stupendous rocks, and then came down to hold the Council meeting where the center of the Wheel had been. We dedicated the Pipe R. had given me, which descended to him through a relative who believed it was an ancient Blackfoot Pipe broken during the time of "the troubles," as the Irish would say, and rescued by a white colonel. The broken stem of the pipehead will remind us when we smoke in Council, not to break pledges, treaties, words. The stem will be the talking stick.

It was a beautiful ceremony in a very charged, powerful place.

Tuesday, June 17th.

After some false starts we got off and drove through haze and cloudiness which lifted after Bishop. It turned into a gorgeous drive to Monitor and Ebbets Pass. The pass has only just been opened. Everything was cleared and clean and empty of traffic, some of the lakes still under ice and snow. We drove till late afternoon, then parked beside the Carson River, looking silvery and rushing fiercely down. We had our evening Pipes in a clump of trees facing southwest instead of east, because it seemed right to face the river.

Wednesday, June 18th.

Woke by the silver river and drove on up the pass into snowdrifts deep by the roadsides and in the woods and on the mountain tops. It was a magic drive, before the defiling traffic comes. We stopped at a good place for the morning Pipe, using Tioga as a shield, as we smoked on the side of the road overlooking all the countryside. The meditations in the Pipe are naturally for the pilgrimage, and for the Sun Dance. It would be wonderful to be young and dancing, or even old and dancing, but not with these cottonwool legs.

Friday, June 20th.

I had a lovely early morning talk with Dr. G. Peggy and Connie arrived to take Edie to the Solstice celebration. After they had gone I had my Solstice Pipe on the patio and then went in for treatment. Dr. G. gave me a thymus "thrust" as I think of it, as her group began arriving for their weekly session. Almost at once PAIN came in like a tidal wave as it always does with thymus. Everything came alive and after that the pain increased and took over. I traveled out of my overcoat, to confused experiences of dancing with Power Animals.

Saturday, June 21st.

Woke on this solstice day as the sun came up. PAIN still waiting round the corner, ready to spring, and aching steadily. It put me in mind of the pain of the thongs attached through the flesh in the most strenuous form of the Sun Dance. "The stinker!" Dr. G. said about the pain. I said, "Yes—literally—" One can say anything to Dr. G.—anything that is true. I spent the day thinking of the Sun Dance to come and being treated on and off. In the evening we were having our Pipes in the Tioga, to be out of the way of Dr. G. and her Friday evening group, who might need the patio where we usually smoke here. Jim arrived with offerings and gifts, especially a Navaho wind bell. He sat while we smoked and meditated with us. He told me he had set up a rock and a candle for us and would keep them going through the Sun Dance days. He told us the plans for his group, which sound right.

Sunday, June 22nd.

Dr. G. treated me again this morning. Then she came out to the camper and asked me to do a Pipe ceremony for her Sunday group. I took the required three days—translated to three minutes, a day a minute—to agree and went out to the patio. The group was open and harmonious to the Pipe. They received the blessing and the light they were seeking, except for one young man who sat next to me and was full of fear. I spoke to that fear as well as I could, and for some flickering instants felt that he was soothed.

Then we said good-bye and drove away to the Quaker Center. I had some pain and discomfort but I felt more energy that Dr. G. had given me, and was able this evening "to set the tone for the week" as I had undertaken to do. It seemed to go well. It is a good group, and being mainly Catholic sisters, meditation is an old story to most of them. This helps. I devoted half the time to Amerindian poetry and half to explaining the Medicine Wheel, out of *Snowy Earth Comes Gliding*, so that we can devote all the time to the ritual of the Medicine Wheel tomorrow, instead of having to explain it first and cut short the working.

Tuesday, June 24th.

A good Pipe under the great redwood trees. Edie had a specially high one, she said. There was a telephone message from Edward Heyoka about where and how to meet him next week. It doesn't seem quite real to me, that I am on the way to a Sun Dance and invited to be a small but necessary part of it. At 5:00 we had the Medicine Wheel and after it I asked each one to tell what her or his experiences had been. As usual these were different and revealing. I hope they will be able to interpret them and discover where they are now and some of what comes next. I am weak and wobbly but not in too much pain.

Wednesday, June 25th.

Pipe in our usual place under the redwood trees. I had some difficulty with it at first, but then we soared. At 8:00 I held the first Pipe ceremony with the group. It went well. All of them were with it. There was an older nun about whom some of them were anxious. They needn't have been. She said the most with-it things of anyone and later told Edie she was forty-seven years in the Church and *was* the

Church, and so was able to recognize the mistakes the Jesuits made with the Indians.

We chanted a little, not perhaps enough, but time was pressing. I believe they all received as much as they were open to. The moon added her light. That upper chamber with its big windows is a good place to hold gatherings. Our Pipe ceremonies will add to its vibrations. Someone asked how I knew that smudging works. I said it was like incense. How did we know that censing works? They understood that.

Thursday, June 26th.

For the last of my commitments to this group I tried a new experiment, the Medicine Wheel and Pipe combined. I had the people place their stones in front of them, then while we (Edie, T. M and I) smoked, to take thought forms of those whom they wanted to help, into the center and place them there. I took my little sick great granddaughter in, and others. Then we brought the thought-forms out, blessed and released them. When the smoking was over, I asked each to tell what he or she experienced, and it was interesting. Even so brief an experience of the Medicine Wheel brings great results. They now can work on this for themselves.

Friday, June 27th.

Back to Dr. G. for a last check up and treatment. Bob called to say there was a bad motor accident involving four people and would I put them in my Pipe. I said I would. We drove on past Reno and beyond, through green fields and by a lake and on towards Alturus. We found—the Grandfathers found for us—a tree, the only one in a vast expanse of exposure and here we smoked and had supper. Then we drove on to a strange garage sort of place off the highway for the night. I spent a restless night, full moon, trains shunting, but it was a good place and we were glad the Grandfathers found it for us. I had some revealing dreams about releasing fears and guilt.

Saturday, June 28th.

We got away early and drove to the park in Oregon where once before we smoked gentle Pipes by the gentle stream. Then we drove on and on and on for now we must make time if we are to get there when we are expected. We saw deer, an eagle and some hawks, and came on a group of regretful people whose car had just killed a big bird. We thought it was an eagle. We stopped, and when the people had gone, went back to see and to take the body off the highway. It was a glorious huge owl with white fur on its feet, a magnificent undamaged specimen. A taxidermist would have loved it. Its great eyes were open. It was still warm. Its neck was broken. Edie carried it up the rocks and laid it to rest in a rabbit-brush bush, with some sage and an offering of tobacco and, of course, a prayer. Then we drove on, listening to the opera, Leontine Price. (It is good to be a Métis and able to enjoy all kinds of music.) We watched the sun go down and came to a campground by the Snake River.

Sunday, June 29th.

On to Yellowstone, through hundreds of acres of dead and dying trees. What's with the trees? Defoliation karma? Use of Napalm? Our national and racial karma is horrific. We drove on through the northern section of Yellowstone to a small chapel and smoked behind it. Many mosquitoes, but an Eagle came and soared high above us lifting our spirits.

Monday, June 30th.

We got off to an early start for the most awe-inspiring drive through the north end of Yellowstone to Billings. On the way we stopped for the Pipe at a rushing waterfall facing a massive rock. A party of motocyclists arrived, but they stayed away from us, with the torrent in between. Drove on, reaching Hardin at 1:30. Here Edie disappeared into the Safeway for a long time, stocking up a week's supply of food, for we shall not want to leave the Sun Dance camp when once we get there. We had a hard time finding it, being misdirected several times by sullen or scornful Indians. Tioga gives the impression of rich tourists, instead of the office-ambulance of a sick and not-at-all-rich woman and her sustainer-companion. We were sent to Tom Yellow Tail's house, and there met with two tactiturn young men, one white, one red. They told us that everyone was up at the Sun Dance, and mentioned Grass Lodge, which we had passed several times. We went back there, and I got out to ask an older and very disinterested Indian where the Sun Dance was? When he didn't answer I said, "I am Grandmother to one of the dancers." Then he said, "The Sun Dance is over." I said, "I don't think so. It doesn't start till the second. Chief Tom Yellow Tail. . . ." "Oh that dance," he said. "Over there." He waved vaguely toward the horizon, and closed his eyes. While we pondered where to go next, a huge machine with a long pole on it, turned on an uphill path ahead of us. Behind it came a procession of cars. "The Tree! They're bringing in the Tree!" Our hearts lifted at the sight of it, the sacred Center Pole ritually escorted. We joined in at the tail end of the procession and arrived in perfect timing, to Heyoka's delight, who was waiting for us. We camped behind his colorful tipi, next to the Medicine Man's tent. This first night we ate with the Medicine Man and his sweet ill wife and three young men in the central tent. Alas, they ate nothing but slabs of over-cooked Safeway steaks, store-bought buns, white sugar and coffee. They were very contemptuous of vegetarians. What the conquerors have done to the conquered doesn't bear thinking of. So many of what was and still sometimes is, a strong and healthy race, are now obese and ill. All because the food is wrong, and they have been encouraged to follow bad examples. After the meal and a little shy talk and long silences, we withdrew to Tioga.

We were on a promontory, with Edward's tipi in front of us, the Medicine Man's tents to our right, and a thin line of tents beyond that. Below us the long meadow stretched, where the Sun Dance Lodge would be set up and the ceremony take place. It was nothing but an empty field as yet. There was no one camped to our left so we felt that we could have our evening Pipes outdoors shielded on the right by Tioga, but under the wide sky, with the Sun Dance site laid out before us to be blessed. First, of course, I followed the rules of courtesy. This was Chief Yellow Tail's territory. I told him I was a Pipe Carrier, and asked if we might smoke our Pipes in the ways we were accustomed to, while we were there. He said yes. The Crows, I learned later, are not particularly devoted to the Pipe, except for occasional use. They make their prayers and offerings of tobacco through cigarettes. This may be one reason for what followed.

Midway in the smoking two cars spurted up beside us on the left. Men, women and kids spilled out of them and began to stake out camping places very near us. They did not see us at first, they were busy unloading things and shouting to and fro. When they did see us instead of respectful silence, appreciation and perhaps a little friendly wave, they began to jeer, to hoot with laughter, and to say obviously scornful things, in Crow. Again it may have been the misleading image of Tioga, but even if they thought we were white tourists, our attitude and our occupation should have registered. The barrage of mockery and hostility lasted a long time. Meanwhile we continued, shaken, and saddened, to finish the ceremony. I asked forgiveness of the Grandfathers for exposing the Pipes to this pollution. When we had finished and put away the sacred objects, we went inside and drew down our curtains. It will be unpleasant to have these particular neighbors so close to us. One wonders why they are coming to the Sun Dance.

Tuesday, July 1st.

The setting up of the Tree and the building of the Lodge is going on below. Only those who have been appointed to serve in this way may go near. It is a strange day, very hot and muggy. Tioga with all the windows open is the best place to be. Now and then we go to sit with others at the communal table outside the Medicine Man's tent. A long corridor of poles with branches across them for shade runs the whole length of the camp, each tent constructing its own part of it. Here people eat and talk and renew or make friendships. There are only a handful of whites, here by special invitation, among them a young French writer, Pierre, from Normandy. We talk for awhile in French, with some nostalgia. He asks me to be his Grandmother for the dancing too. The few Whites, or rather Métis, though they may not know it yet, adopt Tioga as their home from home and are in and out of it. Steve and Gina are colleagues at the same college and linked with the St. George Homes, in fact we met them there. Steve is a young novelist finishing his first book. Heyoka, his wife and three children are in and out. So are various dogs and babies. Edie rises valiantly to feeding and caring for all who come.

We talk and I learn a lot, especially from Heyoka. This Crow Sun Dance is different from the others I have studied, in many ways. They don't pierce the flesh. The ties attaching each dancer to the center pole are spiritual thongs, attached to the same place, below the breast, that the physical thongs would be. The dancing is different, since spiritual thongs allow more freedom of movement. The dancers rush towards the Pole, and at some point touch it, then they toe-heel, toe-heel, back to their places at the outer edge of the circle. They have eagle plumes on their wrists, and eagle whistles, like the other attached dancers, which they blow all the time that they dance. They break off from dancing at intervals and are allowed to sleep between times.

The hostile people next door went away after setting up their camp and will not be back until tomorrow night when the opening dance begins the four night ceremony, so we can have our Pipe outdoors.

Wednesday, July 2nd.

We rose before dawn and got ready for the Pipe, inviting Heyoka to join us, since it was for him. Joan (his wife) and the youngest child joined us too. The sun came up at the highest moment. My tobacco was damp, the Pipe sang a little chant of its own. A long hot day followed of waiting for the opening dance tonight. Meanwhile many tents had been set up on both sides of the canyon, the miniature valley where the Dance is being held. There are about two hundred people here already, and a hundred dancers, men and women, among them four non-Indians, students of the Medicine Man's, although I don't suppose they are so "non" as all that. They are Métis. The Crows seem to be all Crow. They speak, adults and children, only the Crow language. We hear no English as we go about. It is impressive to see and move among so large a group so integrated, so at home, at ease in their own culture. We hear that much has deteriorated in the tribe here, as everywhere, but still, visibly so much lives.

After the long hot day of watching gradual, almost imperceptible changes taking place below, darkness surrounded us, and still the opening dance had not begun. The climb down is steep and difficult for me, my "standing behind" Edward is well begun and tonight I am not needed to be physically present yet. Edie went down, but I gave up, and heard the drumming and the chanting while I smoked my Pipe for an auspicious opening. Drumming is in my blood. It takes me completely over. The first beats made me realize, drove it into me, that I was about to partake of a Sun Dance, tolerated if not exactly welcomed, but a part of it, and rightly here. I lay and listened and shivered. Edie came back and described what she had seen. It was midnight before we got bedded down.

Thursday, July 3rd.

We rose at dawn and saw activities beginning. Edie rushed out and saw the double rainbow blessing the start. I came later. We stood respectfully behind the little group being instructed by the Medicine Man. Then we went back and had our Pipes in Tioga—impossible to have them outdoors now, even though the hostile neighbors have not reappeared, it is still too public. A long wait followed. I found an opportunity to speak to the Medicine Man, whom everybody seems to call Tom. I gave him my offering, and told him my predicament, and asked for his blessing. He looked sad, said nothing, but nodded my dismissal. A little later he came out of his tent and stared anxiously toward the West, where another rainbow was forming. He frowned, murmured something. Edward standing near told me that the rainbow was in an ominous part of the sky. It was not a good omen for the dance. Presently the sky darkened and a sudden fierce wind, which for a few moments seemed like a hurricane, blew over us. Down went many tents. Those of the hostile neighbors were completely flattened and all their belongings were scattered over the hillside. When they returned, ready to settle in, and saw what had happened, they gathered up their things, drove away and never came back. I felt for them. Pierre's little pup tent went down. Heyoka's tipi writhed to left and right but stood up firmly. So did "Tom's" tent with people holding ropes to help. But a little further to the right of us several tents went down. There had been some drinking there we heard. Tom came out. The wind died away. Another rainbow appeared right over the Sun Dance Lodge. With the clearing of the sky, Tom's face cleared too. He smiled. He is a very awesome man, gentle but extremely strong, no one to tangle with or to call "Tom" to his face. He is the nearest thing I can imagine to an Egyptian High Priest of the uncorrupted days. He stood looking toward the rainbow for a time and then disappeared into his tent.

We felt the Grandfathers had given a warning demonstration and taken care of the trouble spots, the obviously not-with-it people, and that now those who were here for the right reasons would enter more deeply into the sacrifice, for it is that, a Dance of Renewal, first of those who set it in motion, then the family, the tribe, the nation, the land, the world. It is set in motion to fulfill a vow made by an individual, but it requires the cooperation of a large group to bring it to its great conclusion. We had met and talked to the man who was sponsoring this Sun Dance, providing all the food, among other Give-Aways, and found him a sensitive fine person, caring deeply for everyone present.

So far this has been a very Indian gathering, a slow-flow, but everything gets done surprisingly quickly and surely. Turn your eyes away for a moment, it seems, and more of the Lodge is up, or the Pole and the sacred objects are suddenly in place, yet nothing seems to be happening for long stretches of waiting. So far it hasn't seemed the high, holy, serious occasion for everyone that we expect. It is a mixture of noise and sociabilities and confusion and bad eating and junk and simplicity and sincerity and beauty. The dance itself and everything about it is fine and pure. The Lodge is perfect. This Medicine Man is a beautiful, wise being, but the children shout and scream and race about at the most sacred moments. People crowd where they have just been told not to go. A child (and probably more than one) touched the Buffalo Skull and the sacred Eagle, though we had all been warned never to desecrate them by touching them. Perhaps another reason for

that Sudden Wind. But tonight the going-in ceremony and the scene under the stars was so moving,
so lifted out of the context of this world, that everyone was silenced, and the real event began. The
colors of the dancers' skirts—the men had four, one
for each night's wearing—were so intricately composed of gloriously bright colors that one could only
think of peacocks and quetzal birds and exotic flowers. The women's belts and dresses were almost as
colorful; for there were women dancers as well as
men. Most of them were elders with strong and beautiful faces, the beauty that comes with hard lives and
wisdom, but there were some young and pretty faces
too. We could only see the interior of the Lodge by
crowding round the entrance to the East and taking
turns at peeking. In front of the "door" the drummers, eight of them around an enormous drum, and a
group of women singers, made peeking difficult, but
we saw, we swallowed, we heard, the senses were
deeply satisfied, the spirit soared in marveling praise
to Wakan-Tanka, Creator and Source of All That Is.

Friday, July 4th.

Rose with the sun. Edie went down for the sunrise
ceremony. I had the Pipe for that and for my grandsons, Edward and Pierre. Their places are side by
side. They rush in toward the Tree together, in their
group, and back again to their places. The dancers
have their sleeping bags in the spaces behind them
and can rest between times, while other groups
dance. There is not room for all the hundred at once.
I went down in the heat of the day to support
Heyoka. He was dancing well, with plenty of energy. Pierre was pacing himself more slowly. I did
what I was supposed to do for each of them, and
stayed down in the heat of the day, watching the

ceremony, dancing in my heart to the drumming and the chanting. The drummers and the singers kept it up without a pause except for the brief rests at prescribed break-off times. Their participation is as strenuous as the dancers', except that they may drink water which is brought to them. The dancers are enduring thirst. We drink for them, eat for them, sleep for them, and send them energies. Toward evening a wind came up to cool things off a little. We climbed back to the camp. We can hear the drumming well from Tioga. It is very evident the power is building up.

Saturday, July 5th.

This is the day when the dancers need the most help. We went down early and stood where they could see us and know that we were praying for them. We went round behind the Lodge and knelt close to the brush separating us from their resting places, and talked encouragingly. Later my great moment came. People were lining up at the entrance to go into the circle for healing from the Medicine Man. His wife told me to stand in line and she would tell me when to go forward. I waited a long time, conscious of curious glances, some of them suspicious and cold. Several times during the days and nights here I was made to realize again that I do not feel comfortable with people who judge me by what they think they see of my envelope or know of my background. This is why I do feel comfortably at home in Nama. No Métis can look askance at another Métis for differences of pigmentation or background. For unworthy behavior, yes. But Nama includes "all our relatives." Ultimately Nama should include all sentient creatures on our Mother Earth.

At last the signal came. I took off my hat and shoes

and walked in alone to the high and holy place I had watched from the outside for three days. I was the last to enter. There were to be no more healings. I stood at the end of the line while the Medicine Man doctored women and babies. One by one they left the circle. Then he turned to me and told me to face the East and put both hands on the pole, a tall pole, painted blue, with the sacred Otter on top of it. I did so and found myself looking out through the opening I had looked in from, and immediately the faces of the crowd faded. An extraordinary well-being flooded me. I cannot describe what began to happen next. I was conscious that I was being honored with a special attention. No one else had been doctored in this way at the Pole. I was at the center of the Circle, with the Tree near me and my hands on the supporting Medicine Rod. Something deep and timeless was taking place within and without. I heard the Medicine Man's voice behind me telling me to "do my talking," i.e. to pray. I began to cry out for help and to give thanks for the help that I was receiving, as the great healing feather swept across the pain area and took the pain away. Now the Medicine Man signaled to the drummers and the singers. Their response crescendoed, though it didn't seem possible it could get any louder.

The dancers rushed in towards me as I stood leaning on the Pole. I began to understand more of the tremendous build-up of power in the center of the Sun Dance Lodge. It surged in with the dancers, as they ran forward, piping their eagle whistles, waving their eagle plumes. It receded as they toe-heeled, toe-heeled back to their places, and then rushed in again like breakers surrounding a small rock. I felt crowned, sated, deeply healed, at peace.

It was time to leave. I felt my hands being lifted

from the Pole. I turned to this great Medicine Man, Tom Yellow Tail, stammering thanks for the blessing he had given and I received. As we stood facing each other, he looked the venerable Egyptian High Priest I feel he must have been.

Sunday, July 6th.

We were up at 4:30 for the sunrise service and the coming out of the dancers. It was very beautiful. We managed to have ringside seats looking through the entrance. Both the grandsons were up and dancing well, though some of the others did not rouse, and presently the older women rushed to dance and shamed the laggards into getting on their feet. Tom Yellow Tail came forward to the fire. His chants were gentle, penetrating, with the ring of authority and triumph. The fasting days and nights had taken their toll, but he was unconquerable, and he had brought the great rite through all its vicissitudes to a right conclusion.

Heyoka joined us. We went up the hill to socialize and say goodbye. This too was good, though we were none of us quite back on the ground. The village was disappearing as fast as it had gone up five days before. All signs of occupancy were gone. Only those were staying who were appointed to take down the Lodge and smooth over the place where it had been, pile high the still-green boughs of the walls and roof and cart them away, leaving only the central Tree, stripped of its sacred objects, to stand until time and winds would bring it down. There were two other trees from earlier dances still standing where their Lodges had been.

We rolled away towards the mountains. We were making for an ancient Medicine Wheel Heyoka told us about, discovered by ancestors of the Crows, and reputed to be thousands of years old. We found that it was indeed a strange and potent place, but there were tourists there so we couldn't smoke our Pipes as we had planned. The ground was covered with spring flowers. It was as high as that. We drove on downward to Rock Creek campground by the river, and settled in there to smoke by the rushing water in a private place. I am thinking over and going back to the timeless moments at the blue Pole in the center of the Sun Dance.

Monday, July 7th.

We drove to a high place on Bear Tooth Pass, from which we could see the entire circle of mountains, and here we greeted the sunrise, then drove on through high tundra country, Edie looking hopefully for big horn sheep. We stopped by a mountain lake for breakfast. Flowers everywhere, kinds that I don't know, mosquitoes everywhere too, so we can't go out, but Tioga, bless the faithful sturdy truck, has many vistas. The rest of the journey was beautiful and new to us. When we stopped for the night and smoked our Pipes the wind came up and sang and talked to us. I heard words but couldn't understand them. We talked of the Sun Dance and remembered it together. I feel healed and hopeful. It will be interesting to hear what Dr. G. finds when I get there. I know some great change has taken place in me. It was a crowning.

🔳🔳🔳🔳

1981 was the year that I was invited to participate in three public Great Medicine gatherings sponsored by Sun Bear, and to bring my helpers. I do not have an organized group, a community, like many Medicine People. People come and go like flocks of migrating birds. Some want to be students, some are patients, some come for specific reasons, recommended by others, and always my—in other systems she might be called "chela," but I do not accept chelas—Edie, who since 1974 has accompanied me, taking care of the nitty gritty around this sick and aging human overcoat, requiring at times much help and care. There is also my daughter, Terry, the official singer in our Sweat Lodge, and others who come with steady persistence and can be called on for help. Many of these have Pipes.

With these supporters I set out for the gatherings, not sure of what the Grandfathers wanted from me. The first took place near Los Angeles, at the Calamigos Star C. Ranch in the Malibu Mountains, on May 22, 23 and 24. It was co-sponsored by the Bear Tribe Medicine Society; the Deer Tribe Medicine Society; with support from the Hutash Community of Human Dimensions Institute West, Ojai; The Heartlight Community, Calabasa; The Healing Light Center of Glendale; and NAMA, the National American Métis Association, of which I am the "wizened" tribal grandmother. I like being "wizened." It reminds me of Merlin. It adds a touch of magic and of color to the exacting business of being a bridge between so many different degrees and kinds of people.

Thursday, May 21st, 1981.

We drove through beautiful Walker Pass, Kern, etc. and down Highway 99 (pah!) for awhile, and across to 33 and through the Los Padres National Forest. There is a ghouly feeling of alarming hostile vibrations in many parts of Los Padres. We struck one of those at twilight and drove through it, not wanting at all to stop, but we did have to stop for the night, choosing some higher ground, with a tremendous view, and after a Pipe in Tioga, we felt protected and able to keep apprehension at bay.

Friday, May 22nd.

We woke in this stupendous place high up over the world, and had a grateful Pipe here for protection in the night, blessing the countryside, our duty as Pipe Carriers. A hawk made its presence felt, otherwise all was silent, except for occasional cars. One stopped, but I don't think they saw us. They just needed a blessing, as often happens on the road. We drove on through Ojai, by spring-flower ways. The countryside was very alive. Eventually we arrived at the sea and went down the coast to Malibu and up Mulholland Drive. We found the gathering place and were a little taken aback at the milling crowds with an out-for-a-good-time look about them and very little visible with-it high. A man on a spirited little horse was directing traffic and attending to parking. He put us in a spot "near where the ceremonies will be," but also cheek by jowl with other campers and no privacy. We had hardly turned off the motor, prepared to make the best of the niche allotted to us, when Mary Shy Deer arrived to say that we had our reserved place by the Staff Lodge up the hill. It was a case of "Friend go up higher." We found ourselves in a private corner by a great gnarled tree whom I shall not forget. One side of her was a naked demure naiad and the other a screaming harridan. If you moved a little this way or that you got views of this dichotomy in the being who was to be our nearest neighbor for the weekend. People came to greet us. We ate with the crowd in the communal dining hall. This was somewhat disconcerting. I sat next to a woman who worked for a company manufacturing talking toys. She had seen the announcement in the newspaper and come because she "was always interested in new ways of communication." Then she asked: "Will there by anything about Indians?" I said "Yes indeed, I suppose so," and made for the terrace, wondering if this was the general level of benevolent ignorance we were to deal with. My Sun Dance grandson Heyoka introduced me to Rainbow Hawk, an older Medicine Man from Costa Rica, with whom I felt instant love and understanding.

Saturday, May 23rd.

We had the morning Pipe in Tioga. Terry came. We all went up together to Sun Bear's opening Pipe Ceremony, which was impressive and powerful. Afterwards all the speakers spoke, I among them. I don't remember very well what I said. I smudged with the young people, and explained it to the crowd, and said a prayer—"did my talking to the Grandfathers." Then we all went to different corners to hold our seminars. Mine developed into healings. I held two healing ceremonies the first session, and three the next. We could have spent a month on these. In the afternoon everyone participated in setting up the big Medicine Wheel round which everything important will take place.

Sunday, May 24th.

We had a wonderful Pipe with Heyoka and the Costa Rica Medicine Man, Rainbow Hawk—very close companionship. Then I went up as asked to open the second session. I could not use my Pipe as had been suggested, but I had my helpers chant with me, and I prayed and blessed the audience. We honored Sun Bear by singing the Bear Song. Then came the seminars, mine on the Medicine Wheel, followed by healings. After that I listened to Brad Steiger and

Page Bryant, both excellent speakers. After lunch, which Terry brought to me beneath the trees, I held another session with healings, and later took part in the Give-Aways and the last ceremonies. The whole gathering was interesting on many levels. It is a new experience to share one's inner life with three hundred and fifty people, and to watch the changes come over them as they absorb the teachings and participate in the ceremonies. There have been breakthroughs and changes in many lives. We watched the exodus, a very different crowd from the one we saw arriving. Soon the whole site was empty except for the staff and Sun Bear's group and us and Rainbow Hawk.

Monday, May 25th.

Woke early and had another Pipe where we had one yesterday, with Heyoka and Rainbow Hawk. The tree revealed herself as the sun came out over her head and filtered down to us. Grandfather Crow came to bless us. Friendships were cemented and plans made for the future. The impressive thing for me was the exposure of so many people to a better, more truthful view of "Indians" and Native-American culture, one that didn't shut them out but took them in, opening the vista and the promise before them of alternative ways to those they feel themselves trapped in. We don't have to accept what others decide for us. We don't need to feel helpless in the hands of specialists and authorities. Even in a hospital, where the moment we are horizontal we lose our individuality and our control over our destinies, we do not have to submit meekly to what is decided for us. We have rights, and the most important is the right to decide for ourselves what is to be done to us.

Before becoming statistics with irrelevant opinions over what is vitally important to us, we should explore other ways of dealing with our problems, other ways of living, other ways of discovering what is true. The vested interests who take "in God we trust" on the dollar bill to mean God *is* the dollar, would have us believe that they have the monopoly on the regulation of our lives, and our deaths; that if we are healed of cancer, say, in any way but theirs, which seldom heals, we have fallen into the hands of quacks, or else we never had cancer in the first place, it was a mistaken diagnosis, in spite of all the expensive tests.

There are thousands today who can bear witness to the alternative ways of healing and to combinations of them. Wholistic healing covers a wide range, which is coming more and more into the limelight. When I come down from the mountain, back from the Medicine Wheels and other seminars and gatherings, and there are more and more people waiting to show their cancers, cancers of spirit, of mind, of heart, affecting their heavy human overcoats, I tell them that all healing comes from Wakan-Tanka through the healing Grandfathers and dedicated channels, and that they have each of them their own greatest Healer the Great Spirit within. I bless them with crystal, feather, herbs; I give them the courage I so nearly didn't have; I tell them to renounce the negativities, they must have no doubts, no fears, and no self-pity; they must turn from poisons, poisonous drugs, poisonous habits of thought and behavior. They must search out the many avenues now opening for them, and find the one, or combination of healing ways, which is the way for them. Nowadays there are doctors even in the A.M.A. who understand that healing takes place at spiritual levels.

Many chiropractors also base their healing methods on this truth, which has always formed part of their training. I tell them what I have discovered of Wholistic healing, and if it ever becomes legal in this country as it is in Europe, of radionics and other methods beginning to be understood, and especially the re-emergence of the native American ritual healings.

Finally I give them a prescription which never fails —once a day at least make someone, especially yourself, laugh in a joyful kindly way. Kindly laughter is good medicine. Above all we must work with the imagination, our irresistible sure instrument to bring about the good conditions we desire for others and ourselves. This is another way of saying to implement the will of the Creator, Source of all blessings.

"Atomic power is nothing compared to the power of the dream that lives in each of us that is seeking emergence."[25] Even on this plane those who take part in peaceful demonstrations against "spiritual wickedness in high places," as Saint Paul puts it, know this to be true.

The second Medicine Wheel gathering took place in August near Seattle, and was remarkable because it was steadily rained upon and no one seemed to mind and no one left. Little pup tents were soggy. Shelters when there were any, dripped. Seminars took place in misty soakings. But everyone persisted, faces shone, we gave thanks for the rain falling on the thirsty land. People were healed, relationships were strengthened, new bridges made, and the ceremonies around the Medicine Wheel were strong and impressive.

The third Medicine Wheel, the first one held in the Bay Area, came in October. It had the largest atten-

25. David Spangler, *Revelations*.

dance, almost a thousand people, and was held among the redwood hills of Camp Royaneh near Cazadero. The ceremony of building the Medicine Wheel was enhanced by the cooperation of masked dancers from the Rites of Passage representing Mother Earth, Grandmother Moon, Grandfather Sun, the Turtle, Frog, Bear and Eagle Clans, each carrying a rock to form the circle round the sacred Buffalo skull, placed in position by Sun Bear. Other dancers followed, with rocks for the twelve moons, different clans, qualities, etc. When the inner circles were completed many hundreds formed the outer circumference, each with a stone or rock.

"In our philosophy," Sun Bear pointed out, "we feel that each person has something to contribute to the whole. No one has all the answers. At grand Medicine Ceremonies we come together to share, to grow, and to help each person to become a more balanced human being."

As the tribal grandmother, I was called on to take part in many of the blessings, and to open and close some of the sessions, as well as taking care of the workshops I was expected to lead. It is a challenge to be Grandmother. King Solomon said we should pay heed to the wisdom of the elders. This is beginning to be recognized among the people aware of the new era into which we are moving. Not long ago, and still in the mass of those who cling to the Piscean age, to be an elder was to be a bore, a has-been, of no value or possible interest to the young. Now to be an elder is to have a large family of hungry grandchildren, avid for counsel and for listening ears, and, of course, for unpossessive love. It is a great challenge. An Elder must have wisdom, and be willing and able to share it, to be entitled to respect.

I have always felt that we should build on what has

been transmitted to us through the ages, that we do not, like the ants, have to begin again every generation, from scratch. I believe in a wide use of quotations. If someone before us, laboring, as all artists must, to produce perfect content in perfect form, has managed to say something well we should honor that artist's words by giving them an extension of attention, of life-span. We should learn them by heart when they touch our hearts, quote them to others, linger over them in meditation. Therefore in the next few pages we are concerned with what a wide range of people have wanted to give us—their Give-Aways to generations following them, concerned with their concerns.

We should make our own anthologies, as we should keep our own log-books, even though nothing that we say or do or read or can remember does justice to the wisdom growing within. Reminders of this kind link us with others, and reassure us that we are not alone, or strange, or even crazy, as our lower selves sometimes whisper, in holding to the truths we discover. We join the company of the best and clearest minds of all the ages.

This is especially valuable and comforting when there comes a shift in the perspective of the journey. Underneath the busy river of my days and nights, there flowed another stretch of water, widening to the sea. While the lower levels of my mind apparently functioned as usual and I appeared to see and hear whatever was brought to my attention, the rest of me was haunted by voyages in boats.

First there was the ark, with childish memories, pictures, stories and of course the Noah's Ark into which I put more than the animals. Later deeper memories surfaced.

Both on the material and the spiritual planes the ark symbolizes the power to preserve all things and to ensure their rebirth.

Rebirth is the quest we are all concerned with.

Biologically speaking the ark can be regarded as a symbol of the womb or of the heart. . . . The basic symbolism of the ark is the belief that the essences of the physical and spiritual life can be extracted and contained within a minute seed until such time as a rebirth creates the conditions necessary for the re-emergence of these essences into external life. Guénon has found subtle analogies, of great symbolic interest, between the ark and the rainbow. The ark during the cosmic pralaya floats on the waters of the lower ocean; the rainbow, in the realm of the 'upper waters,' is a sign of the restoration of the order which is preserved below in the ark. Both figures together, being complimentary, complete the circle of Oneness.[26]

The circle of Oneness is another name for the Medicine Wheel round which we progress. As to the rainbow, there was a rash of rainbows at this time over my home, my Sweat Lodge, my travelings, accompanied by quotations:

My heart leaps up when I behold
A rainbow in the sky.

                                        Wordsworth

I took it for a faery vision
Of some gay creatures of the element
That in the colors of the rainbow live
And play in the plighted clouds.

                                        Milton

---

26. J. E. Circlot, *A Dictionary of Symbols* (New York: Philosophical Library, 1972).

Look upon the rainbow and praise Him who
  made it.

Ecclesiasticus

The poet will follow the rainbow.

O'Reilly

Shimmering with the rainbow hues of song.

Realf

We have a secret that doth show us
Wonderful rainbows in the rain.

Anonymous

The combination of *rain* and *bow* opens vistas of speculation I would like to have time to pursue, but the quotation I often read and keep handy to quote is the vision of Vinson Brown, a contemporary Métis Wise Man who also believes in quotations and has written inspired books.

> Slowly a bow formed in the sky, a rainbow of people marching to glory, a rainbow of unity and a vision so marvelous in its sense of beauty and joy that I can never forget it nor hope to see anything its equal. Slowly at the end of each dream this vision of glory would fade away, but the promise of it always remained, the promise of a wonderful change coming.[27]

The change will come for us only if we set out for it, only if we believe in it.

In what torn ship soever I embark,
That ship shall be my emblem of Thy ark.

John Donne
(At the Author's Last Going into Germany)

---

27. William Willoya and Vinson Brown, *Warriors of the Rainbow* (Happy Camp, Naturegraph, 1962).

The journey is always a vision quest, even when it seems to be a terrestrial passage from one place to another, as Donne's "At the Author's Last Going into Germany" or an epic this-plane voyage of Ulysses, Jason and other classic fairy-tale heroes and adventurers.

> So on the deep and open sea I set
> Forth with a single ship and that small band
> Of comrades that had never left them yet. . . .
>
> With our poop shouldering the dawn, we plied
> Making our oars wings . . .
>
> > Dante, "Inferno," Canto VIII,
> > Dorothy Sayers translation.

On coins a ship ploughing through the seas is emblematic of joy and happiness. But the most profound significance of navigation is that implied by Pompey the Great in his remark: "Living is not necessary, but navigation is"—living which he understood as living for or in oneself, and sailing or navigating, by which he understood living in order to transcend.

> . . . every vessel corresponds to a constellation. The ship symbol has been related to the holy island, in so far as both are differentiated from the amorphous and hostile sea. If the waters of the oceans are symbolic of the unconscious, they also can allude to the dull roar of the outside world . . . it is essential first to learn to sail the sea of the passions in order to reach the Mountain of Salvation. For this reason the attainment of the Great Peace is depicted in the form of sailing the seas.
>
> > Dictionary of Symbols

> As in a ship convey us o'er the flood.
>
> > Rig Veda

And he (Noah) said: Embark therein! In the name
of God be its course and its mooring.

Qur'an XI. 41

Shut out worldly sights from your mind with en-
deavor and the utmost perseverance, and cross
the perilous ocean of woe, which is the world, in
the firm barque of your virtues.

Yoga Vasishtha

The pranava (the syllable OM) is like a ferry for
the human beings who have fallen into the boundless ocean of the life of this world. Many have
been able to cross the ocean of deaths and rebirths
by means of this ferry.

Swami Sivananda

Rare indeed is this human birth. The human body
is like a boat, the first and foremost use of which is
to carry us across the ocean of life and death to the
shore of immortality. The Guru (Shaman) is the
skillful helmsman; divine grace is the favorable
wind. If with such means as these man does not
strive to cross the ocean of life and death, he is indeed spiritually dead.

Srimad Bhavagatum

The journey is full of perils to which all those who
have attempted it attest.

Many great storms and temptations, peradven-
ture, shall rise in this time, and thou knowest
never whither to run from sorrow. All is away
from thy feeling, common grace and special. Be
not overmuch afraid then, although thou have
matter (reason) as thou thinkest, but have a lovely
trust in our Lord . . . for he is not far.

An Epistle of the Privy Council

The soul in its frail barque is launched on the wide
ocean, underneath an empty-seeming sky. Never-
theless, courage! We must sail on alone. afraid—in
faith. We must sail on in memory of the Light

which we have known, seen, loved, for however
short a time, and lost, it seems, irreparably. Erect
in our small boats, between black waves and
blacker sky, let us remember Isis in her night.

E.E. "The Hours of Isis"

He encounters grave difficulties on his way, for
the waves of the ocean are nothing compared with
those of the mind.

Swami Sivananda

Adrift! A little boat adrift!
And night is coming down.
Will no one guide a little boat
Unto the nearest town?

Emily Dickinson

Oh God be good to me! Thy sea is so wide and my
boat is so small.

Breton Fisherman's Prayer

To all at length an end!
All sailors to some unseen Harbour float.
Farewell, mysterious, happy, twilight boat.
Farewell my friend!

Edmund Gosse "The Vanishing Boat"

Each of us has an inherited or developed concept
of that Harbour, that Mountain of Salvation, that
Great Peace, that Abode, that land of stableness, that
haven of health, Jerusalem the Golden, the Happy
Hunting Grounds . . .

The sely soul, at the likeness of a ship, attaineth at
the last to the land of stableness, and to the haven
of health.

Medieval, Anonymous

The world is my sea, the sailor the spirit of God.
The boat my body, the soul he who wins back his
Abode.

Angelus Silesius

I am going a long way
With these thou seest . . .
To the island-valley of Avilion,
Where falls not hail, or rain, or any snow,
Nor ever wind blows loudly, but it lies
Deep-meadowed, happy, fair with orchard lawns
And bowery hollows crowned with summer sea,
Where I will heal me of my grievous wound.
So said he, and the barge with oar and sail
Moved from the bank, like some full-breasted
  swan
That, fluting a wild carol ere her death,
Ruffles her pure cold plume, and takes the flood
With swarthy webs.

> Tennyson "Morte d'Arthur"

The swan with gondoliering legs . . .

> Marianne Moore

These accounts by poets and wise ones centuries and continents apart agree in so many essentials, in their general attitudes and convictions, that they bear witness to the existence of the universal blueprint, the Cosmic Medicine Wheel, behind all creation.

With this wealth of wisdom and reassurance from the Enlightened to guide us we should build our own spirit boats, unique and beautiful and sturdy for the Great Journey. There will be flotillas of all shapes and sizes, from the small canoe carrying one or two, to the sailboat carrying several, to the Ocean liner transporting hundreds, on their different courses, at their different speeds, bound for the same Harbor, differently envisioned. The important thing is to set out boldly, and keep on keeping on.

I started to create my spirit canoe when Dr. G. gave me a rug. It reminded us both of the magic carpet the little lame prince traveled on, in a favorite childhood book we both enjoyed, as contemporaries with different sets of memories, who share some unexpected ones.

It was an ancient hand woven rug with a design that resembled the beaded pattern on a ceremonial collar a Paiute Elder made for me. She said it was "the Medicine Man with his people," but when I saw the same pattern spread on the floor of my private meditation corner, I realized it was a stylized boat, with prow and stern and seats for many "relatives." I put rocks, crystals, and other minerals and medicine objects in the places I thought seemed to be designed to carry them, and at the prow the figure Eagle Man made and gave me years before, a man with outstretched arms in blessing or invocation, to guide the boat forward. I invited presences I hoped would journey with me, and thus surrounded by Grandparents and Medicine Powers, I embarked.

At first I stayed hesitantly moored to the riverbank. For one thing I had no paddle and for another I did not feel "up to" the adventure. That turn of speech is good, implying that we must rise above our lower selves to undertake anything important.

Wednesday, November 19th, 1980.

The Spirit Canoe carpet-tracing-board is a great help. I set the little man in the prow and watch his graceful back. Then I smoke in the stern, with the image of a paddle growing on the left and Bear Companion on the right, but I think he is more on the riverbank or the wharf. The boat is not actually traveling yet, only *there* and ready to set forth with me in it. The Pipe I keep especially for this is getting stronger and sometimes gently urgent. Ripples murmur, "When the time is right."

If the time of transition seems to be close for me or for others I ask that we may be able to go to the Great Spirit singing, "It is finished in beauty, it is finished in beauty," and that meanwhile we may live and move and have our being and do our work as the Great Spirit would have us live and move and be and do, wherever we are placed. Then I remember my vision of the Shaman and the Medicine Wheel.

Once upon a time there was a Shaman and there was a Medicine Wheel and there was a me and there was a you, going round the Wheel, going into and out of the Wheel, going over and on the Wheel. It began to rotate, then it upended, then the Shaman and the me and the you dove through the center together into the Tunnel—not black—a luminous Tunnel, and out of the end of the Tunnel to the shores of a limitless sea. There, after a long time of exploring the shore, we came upon a line of little boats, little spirit cockle-

shell canoes, and we got into them together or separately, and there was a golden path across the water to the setting sun or a silver path to the moon. The password we brought was the old Breton fisherman's prayer: "God be good to me! Thy sea is so wide and my boat is so small."

Those who would, launched out, some erect and singing, others silent, crouching low. They were singing, "It is finished in beauty, it is finished in beauty." Later other words drifted back. They seemed to whisper "In the Beginning? Always a new Beginning . . ." A fleet of little cockleshells, little spirit boats, making toward the Source of All. I blessed them as they went. I told them to go shining.

End Notes

Terry Brengle.
Professional actress, writer, and current production coordinator for Eastern Sierra Television, she is also the author's daughter and the mother of her four grandchildren.

Iren Marik.
Internationally known concert pianist, graduate of the Conservatory of Music and the Franz Liszt Academy of Music in Budapest. Studied with Bela Bartok, George Woodhouse among others. A long and distinguished career includes major concert tours and solo performances with the leading European orchestras, and since 1946 with the National Symphony, Washington, D.C., at Town Hall, New York and numerous cities, including Honolulu, universities and colleges across the United States. Now residing in Independence, California, she is known for the outstanding concert series she performs in the home she shares with the author. Many of her recordings are under the Draco label.

John Ranck.
Made his debut in Town Hall in 1947. Exceptionally fine pianist. In solo recitals throughout America, appearances with orchestra, and on two coast-to-coast tours with Maggie Teyte. With Iren Marik he premiered Messiaen's *Vision des Amens* in America. To-

gether they performed this gigantic piece for two pianos at the Deepest Valley Theatre as described in this book.

Edith Newcomb.
Former Director of the Virginia Center for Creative Arts, long-time friend and associate of the author, without whose generous devotion and support many of the research travels and vision quests would not have been possible.

Métis.
French word specifically the name of a people of French-Indian descent in western Canada. The National American Métis Association is a new organization founded by its president, Hyemeyohst Storm, author of *Seven Arrows* and *Heyokah.* In this context the word Métis has the general meaning of mixed blood. Thus we are all Métis and should all be members of NAMA.

Aim Morhardt.
Painter, composer, writer, living in the Owens Valley.

Aspasia Voulis.
Painter and teacher, fellow of the MacDowell Colony, presently teaching at the Hambidge Foundation, Rabun Gap, Georgia.

Paul Nordoff.
Composer and innovative therapist for autistic and retarded children.

Norma Cordell.
Teacher of the therapeutic qualities of gems, sharing her knowledge and techniques with native "medicine" teachers in New Zealand. Working for the Eugene Center for Healing Arts in Oregon.

Forrest Carter.
Author of *The Education of Little Tree*, account of his childhood in the Appalachian Mountains with his Cherokee-Scottish grandfather and Cherokee grandmother. Also author of *Watch For Me On The Mountain*, a powerful account of Geronimo, the great Apache chieftain and visionary. These two books are musts for those who are attracted to Native American subjects.

Louise Talma.
First woman composer to be made a member of the National Academy of Arts. Composer for Thornton Wilder's opera *Alcestis*. Long list of international and national awards. Student and colleague of Nadia Boulanger at the famous conservatory in Fontainebleau.

Joseph Wood.
Composer and Professor of Music at Oberlin Conservatory of Music. Composed the music for a ballet-oratorio *The Progression*, for which I wrote the text, inspired by the sculptor Blance Dombek's series of wax figures.

Mono Lake
Ecological disaster in the Eastern Sierras, very much in the news in recent years, as its water sources are being drained by the Los Angeles Water and Power Department. It is the vital refueling station for migratory birds, including the rare Phalarope, which are being destroyed, in order to supply Los Angeles with swimming pools, and wasted water.

Deep Springs College.
Small but unusual college on the border of California and Nevada. Founded by Lucius Nunn, who built the first Niagara Falls Power Station and founded Tellu-

ride at Cornell. The students own, manage and run the college as trustees while they are in residence. I was the first writer-in-residence there, and taught for two years as professor of French.

White Eagle.
A name for "wise teacher," and also a name for Saint John. This American Native Indian, member of the White Brotherhood, "spoke" through Grace Cooke, an English medium, for many years. The White Eagle Publishing Trust in Hampshire, England publishes his works. He later "spoke" through an American medium, "Cara," in Connecticut, until her death. Then he came to teach and heal through Mahad'yuni for several years.

Sun Bear.
A Chippewa/Métis medicine man. Received his early training from his uncles, who were medicine men. He began the Bear Tribe in 1970, and his visions and dreams have guided the Tribe through its evolution to become the teaching and healing center it is today. Sun Bear lectures throughout the world on his medicine and visions, the Bear Tribe, Native American philosophy and earth awareness.

QUEST BOOKS
are published by
The Theosophical Society in America,
Wheaton, Illinois 60189-0270,
a branch of a world organization
dedicated to the promotion of the unity of
humanity and the encouragement of the study of
religion, philosophy, and science, to the end that
we may better understand ourselves and our place in
the universe. The Society stands for complete
freedom of individual search and belief.
In the Classics Series well-known
theosophical works are made
available in popular editions.